Mills, Mansions, and Mergers:
The Life of William M. Wood

Edward G. Roddy

Mills, Mansions, and Mergers:

The Life of William M. Wood

Merrimack Valley Textile Museum

NORTH ANDOVER, MASSACHUSETTS

COVER:
Map of Shawsheen Village appears on front cover of
this volume. Reproduced from Plate No. 17, *Atlas of
the City of Lawrence and the towns of Meuthen,
Andover and North Andover, Massachusetts*
(Lawrence, Richards Map Company, 1926). Yellow
indicates wooden buildings, red indicates brick
construction. Note Arden estate, lower left. Back cover
logo is the trade-mark of the American Woolen Company.
(Courtesy of Merrimack Valley Textile Museum)

TITLE PAGE:
William Madison Wood as a young man.
(Courtesy of Merrimack Valley Textile Museum)

Library of Congress Cataloging in Publication Data
Roddy, Edward G., 1921–
    Mills, mansions, and mergers.

    Includes bibliographical references and index.
    1. Wood, William M., 1858–   . 2. Businessmen—
United States—Biography. 3. Textile industry—
United States—History. I. Title.
HD9860.W66R62 1982 338.7′677′00924[B]82-81081
ISBN 0-9374 74-04-5   AACR2

Designed by Klaus Gemming, New Haven, Connecticut
Composed by Finn Typographic Service, Inc.,
    Stamford, Connecticut
Printed and bound by Halliday Lithograph,
    West Hanover, Massachusetts

PRINTED IN THE UNITED STATES OF AMERICA

*Dedicated to the sons and
daughters of the old world
who have enriched America
by their coming to this new land*

FOREWORD

I AM PLEASED that the museum is able to add this biography to its publications list. William Madison Wood is one of the central characters in the industrial history of the Merrimack Valley and a figure of great interest to business and labor historians.

It seems fitting that Wood's biography should be written by Edward G. Roddy, senior historian on the faculty of Merrimack College. The college was founded in 1947 to provide the opportunity for higher education to the descendants of the men and women who produced the cloth that made the valley famous. Although he is an academic historian, Dr. Roddy has written this book primarily for a general adult audience. While other academic historians will discover this is a piece of original research, author and publisher alike hope the book will be read by hundreds of men and women who enjoy biography and local history.

The Lawrence Savings Bank provided the museum with a generous subsidy for the preparation of the manuscript. We are very grateful to Dwain B. Smith, president, for his support.

Thomas W. Leavitt, *Director*
Merrimack Valley Textile Museum

CONTENTS

FOREWORD

I AM PLEASED that the museum is able to add this biography to its publications list. William Madison Wood is one of the central characters in the industrial history of the Merrimack Valley and a figure of great interest to business and labor historians.

It seems fitting that Wood's biography should be written by Edward G. Roddy, senior historian on the faculty of Merrimack College. The college was founded in 1947 to provide the opportunity for higher education to the descendants of the men and women who produced the cloth that made the valley famous. Although he is an academic historian, Dr. Roddy has written this book primarily for a general adult audience. While other academic historians will discover this is a piece of original research, author and publisher alike hope the book will be read by hundreds of men and women who enjoy biography and local history.

The Lawrence Savings Bank provided the museum with a generous subsidy for the preparation of the manuscript. We are very grateful to Dwain B. Smith, president, for his support.

Thomas W. Leavitt, *Director*
Merrimack Valley Textile Museum

PREFACE

In 1975 I engaged in a study of Shawsheen Village in Andover, Massachusetts, sponsored by the Merrimack Valley Textile Museum and funded, in part, by the Massachusetts Foundation for the Humanities and Public Policy. As I researched the origins and the early years (1918–1924) of this model corporate village, I became interested in knowing more about the man who built it. William Madison Wood is a legendary name in New England even today, some sixty-five years after his death. Some of his monuments—the enormous Wood and Ayer Mills of Lawrence, Massachusetts, for example—are scattered about the region. His estate still over-looks Shawsheen Village. Like most legends, however, the Wood tale is a potpourri of fact and fiction. I was told—in all seriousness—"When he came here from Portugal he signed his name with an X," and "He owned so many Rolls Royces that he couldn't count them." I decided that such an individual merited knowing.

In the intervening six years of research, I have learned that Wood is an elusive figure, in death as well as in life. Most of the people who knew him are dead or octogenarians. All of his children are also deceased, and his grandchildren were only tots when he died. Of those who were able to speak knowingly of William M. Wood, most praised him. A few dismissed him as a robber baron. One individual flatly refused to discuss him. Several others smiled and said, "You will never be able to write the full story of Billy Wood." The latter were quite correct. Yet, from the scattered bits and pieces that I have been able to gather in Martha's Vineyard, New Bedford, Lawrence, Andover, and Boston—areas where he lived and worked—there has emerged enough information to make this biography possible.

In researching the life of this textile industrialist, I have incurred more debts than I can ever acknowledge. May these few lines serve as my "thank you note" to one and all.

For research assistance, I am much indebted to Clarisse Poirier, Richard C. Raiche, Dennis M. Toomey, Daniel F. Sullivan, Jr., Carlos Barcelos, the Reverend Timothy Goldrich, Richard C. Kugler, Paul Cyr, Paul Rodrigues, James R. Knott, Joseph A. Canha, Eugene Zepp, Suzanne M. Nault, Muriel Crossman, Pat Amaral, Elinor Reichlin, Christine Boland, Martha Mayo, Maurice Lawzon, Rose-Mary Sargent, and Mark Harrington.

Nancy K. Smith, Town Clerk of Edgartown, and Lena Souza, Assistant City Clerk of New Bedford, were unfailingly kind and thorough in their search of birth and death certificates, tax records, and other public documents.

I am particularly grateful to Cornelius A. Wood, Jr., grandson of William Madison Wood, for making available to me the uncompleted, unpublished autobiography of his father. In no sense, however, is my biography a family-authorized one.

Among several fine people who knew William Wood and who shared their memories in taped interviews, I want to thank by name: Mrs. Ernest Wilkinson (the former Helen Knight), James Dalrymple, James Wallace, Granville Cutler, and the late Raymond "Dick" Hoyer.

I wish to thank the *Essex Institute,* Salem, Massachusetts, for their kind permission to include much of my Shawsheen Village article, which appeared in their *Historical Collections* (April 1982).

Grants from the Merrimack College Faculty Development Fund, the Lawrence Savings Bank, and the Merrimack Valley Textile Museum assisted me in completing the study.

For photographic assistance, my thanks to AnnMarie Manzi, Andover Photo and Advance Reproductions, North Andover.

The staffs of the following institutions deserve my particular thanks: Andover Historical Society; New Bedford Public Library; Boston Public Library; Lawrence Public Library; New England Society for the Preservation of Antiquities, Boston; Cuttyhunk Historical Center; Historical Society of Palm Beach County; Memorial Hall Library, Andover; McQuade Library, Merrimack College; Old Dartmouth Historical Society Whaling Museum, New Bedford, Duke's County Historical Society, Edgartown; Federal Records Center, Waltham; Essex Institute, Salem; Immigrant City Archives, Lawrence; University of Lowell; and Merrimack Valley Textile Museum. Without the holdings of these organizations and the skilled assistance of their staffs, my work would have been impossible.

The back files of the *Andover Townsman* and *New Bedford Standard-Times* proved more than valuable.

To the town and city officials of Andover, New Bedford, Edgartown, Taunton, and Lowell, who patiently bore with me as I requested old and dusty records from their vaults, my sincere thanks.

Two former students, Barbara Carrell and Cathleen Costello, did seminar papers for me on the subject of Shawsheen Village and William M. Wood in 1970. Those papers were perhaps the genesis of this book.

Thomas Leavitt, director of the Merrimack Valley Textile Museum, and Helena Wright, its librarian, have by their encouragement and assistance made my task easier than it might have been.

Peter Ford, a colleague in the Department of History, Merrimack College, has read and commented upon most of the manuscript. I could always count upon his help.

The index was prepared by Gordon Brumm.

Finally, and perhaps most importantly, my special gratitude to Carol P. Raiche and Bronwyn M. Mellquist, whose editing skills and advice in chapter revisions were invaluable.

CHAPTER I

Introduction

WILLIAM WOOD, the son of poor immigrant parents, was born in a small fisherman's cottage in the middle of the nineteenth century. By the time of his death, in the second decade of the twentieth century, he was a member of America's business and social elite. His yearly salary plus commissions of $1,000,000 ranked him as perhaps the second highest paid executive in the United States. His giant textile firm, the American Woolen Company, which he created and dominated for a quarter of a century, was the largest in the world. Several of the mills that he built were the largest of their kind. His fascination with building and architecture culminated in the creation of Shawsheen Village, Massachusetts, an innovative, costly experiment in early twentieth-century American suburban planning.

During his lifetime, William Wood was many things to many people. His family, his friends, and the stockholders of the American Woolen Company admired him for his largesse and healthy dividends. Competitors in the woolen industry saw him as an awesome figure whose decisions could spell survival or disaster. In the minds of labor organizers and some of his workers, Wood was the personification of their crudely-drawn caricature of the robber barons of the wool trust. Others view his leadership in the field of labor/management relations as exemplifying the best in corporate paternalism. In reality, he was all and none of these fancies.

One cannot simply explain him as a product of his times. There were thousands born of similiar backgrounds, who went to their graves unknown and undistinguished. With only the minimum of formal schooling, this son of poor immigrant parents, by dint of hard work, innate ability, driving ambition, and luck, worked his way to the top. Of the countless legends of "rags to riches" which make up America's folklore, few appear more remarkable than the life of William Wood.

In 1858, the year of Wood's birth, English audiences packed halls in London, Oxford, and Cambridge to hear Phineas T. Barnum lecture on "The Art of Money-Getting." In this same year, Horatio Alger, Jr., a student at the Harvard Divinity School, was already toying with the idea of becoming a novelist. It seems fitting that Wood was born in this milieu of the "American Gospel of Success." In his early years, young Wood actually lived out the real-life version of Alger's *Brave and Bold: The Fortunes of a Factory Boy*. During his adult life, he successfully followed the advice that Barnum proffered his audiences.

Tradition has always maintained that every American child inherits, as part of his inalienable birth right, the freedom to shape his own life. Paralleling this concept is the widely held belief that ours is an open society, where birth, wealth, and class do not significantly circumscribe individual possibilities. "The belief that all men, in accordance with certain rules, but exclusively by their own efforts, can make of their lives what they will has been widely popularized for well over a century."[1] That there are dissenters to such national folklore, does not diminish the strong hold this myth has on the popular imagination.

A cluster of economic, intellectual, and religious ideas surround and reinforce this American myth of success. This belief grew and flourished in the United States in the decades following the Civil War, the very years of Wood's youth and early manhood. The roots of the success myth are to be found in American Puritanism. Its Protestant work ethic, with an emphasis on hardwork, frugality, and prudence, viewed a career of business as a divine calling. Ministers often based their sermons on Genesis 47:3, "*What is your Occupation?*" [italics added.] These Anglo-Saxon colonists not only brought Calvinism to New England in their intellectual baggage, they also were embryonic capitalists who believed in private property and the profit motive.

The relation of the success myth to American capitalism was extolled during the late nineteenth century. During these years, the United States rapidly industrialized. In the process, economic conditions produced a great number of millionaires. The very size of some of the fortunes, those of Car-

For one born of such a heritage, there was, in popular American contemporary thought, little hope of advancement into the ranks of the nation's industrial and social leaders. These latter individuals were drawn, with only rare exceptions, from Anglo-Saxon Protestant lineage. They believed themselves the rightful representatives of authority, power, wealth, and Americanism. With the growing surge of immigration from southern and eastern Europe in the latter decades of the nineteenth century, these older Americans created a social and cultural enclave of schools, clubs, and careers that would extend the scope of their power and prestige in American society. By the early twentieth century, this elitist policy was so effective that less than 3 percent of the nation's top business leaders came from immigrant or poor backgrounds.[3] On the contrary, the leading businessmen of the age were usually of colonial ancestry. In their church affiliation, they were Episcopalian, Presbyterian, or Congregational. They had above average educations, came from families connected with business affairs, and possessed a relatively high social standing. The career of an Andrew Carnegie, both poor and an immigrant, was so exceptional that it merely proved the rule. The sign above the door of this exclusive fraternity had words writ large and clear: White, Anglo-Saxon Protestants Only.

Yet, by the early twentieth century, both Andrew Carnegie and William Wood were accepted members of America's business and social elite. Against incredible odds, the Scottish immigrant and the son of Portuguese immigrants, had climbed the American ladder of success. Such is both the myth and reality of American history. In some ways the careers of Carnegie and Wood bear striking resemblances. Both of them were, in their early years, associated with the textile industry. Both started their careers at wages that were anything but spectacular. By dint of hard work, industry, and, yes, luck, they embarked upon their dramatic rise to fame and fortune. Both men were makers of things—manufacturers—not financiers or promoters. "I wish to make something tangible and sell it," wrote Carnegie. He made iron and steel. Wood manufactured woolen and worsted cloth. Business mergers played a major role in the careers of each. These men built mills and mansions and both of them became millionaires who lived regal lives. Carnegie and Wood grew to maturity during the Gilded Age, but they were unusual products of their times.

"When William James labeled success 'the American bitch-goddess,' he was simply paying unwitting tribute to the American dream." The social facts to the contrary notwithstanding, America's belief in the legend of the "rags to riches" self-made man is "sufficient reality unto itself."[4] Wood's life is an in-

negie and Rockefeller, for example, was almost beyond belief. T
of industry dominated the era. Partly because of their conspic
life-styles, this period of American history is known as the Gilde

By 1900, however, the traditional entrepreneurial individu
was the core of the American myth of success, appeared to be a
self-made millionaires were being replaced by the builders of co
talism. "John D. Rockefeller knew of what he spoke, when he
'The day of combination is here to stay. Individualism has g
return.'"[2] It was the beginning of the age of the corporation
economic life. William Wood, nonetheless, managed to succes
both of these worlds. He was a wealthy entrepreneur who saw the
on the wall. In 1899, the year before Rockefeller delivered hi
rugged individualism, William Wood created the first multi-r
corporation in the woolen industry. It was in this same year, 1899
Alger died. It was truly the beginning and the end of an era.

Wood's first real job was in a New Bedford, Massachusetts,
manufacturing concern. Here he sensed the burgeoning of an in
in America. And here, perhaps, the young Wood resolved that
dustry would be his pathway to success. As with Alger, Wood v
in the struggle, in the sheer ability, of young boys of no fortune
not even of any education to speak of), to pull themselves up
bootstraps. For both of these men, courage, hard work, honesty, a
were the necessary ingredients if one was to be a success in the v
ness. In addition, luck, according to the Alger theory, comes
deserve it. It came to Wood in 1888 when he first met the arist
erick Ayer, one of New England's wealthiest men.

The nation's readers wholeheartedly adopted Horatio Alger
advancement. Ministers, educators, and business leaders praised
novels. They believed that young American boys should grow
appreciation of hard work, a strong character, and a belief in
These influential men loved money and power and saw nothi
having and using them. William Wood clearly agreed with thes
exemplified them in his own career.

All the ingredients that Alger poured into his hundred-odd
present in the life of Wood. At the age of twelve, he was forced to
formal schooling and go to work to support his widowed mo
younger siblings. Unlike the young, Anglo-Saxon heroes of A
Wood had an additional handicap: he was the son of Portug
Catholic, immigrants.

triguing facet of this treasured remnant of American folklore. The ingredients are both simple and complex: a son of immigrant parents, fatherless at the age of twelve and self-educated; a young man possessed of an endless curiosity, an abhorrence of waste and inefficiency, and a love of work; a man with driving ambition and luck. These personal traits, set against a background of laissez-faire capitalism, rugged individualism, the Protestant work ethic, and the Horatio Alger work-hard-and-get-ahead syndrome, produce the makings of a remarkable career in American business history. How William Wood managed to gain entry into the temple and worship at the altar of "the American bitch-goddess" is the story that follows.

CHAPTER II

Up the Ladder

LATE nineteenth-century America has been described as "the age of industrial statesmen (or captains of industry)" and, more critically, as "the era of the robber barons." Following the Civil War, the nation enthusiastically embraced industrialization. For ambitious and innovative individuals who correctly gauged the catalytic impact of the parallel forces of urbanization and immigration on industry, there was fame and fortune to be made. Perhaps no other period in our history produced such a varied and remarkable group of entrepreneurs. Their names and their deeds have filled page after page in American history books: Carnegie and Frick in the steel industry, Rockefeller in petroleum, Swift and Armour in meat-packing, Harriman and Hill in railroads, Goodyear and Firestone in the rubber industry, Roebling in bridge building, Morgan in finance, Edison, Bell, and Westinghouse with their inventive genius—the list seems endless and their accomplishments unreal.

William Madison Wood, rightfully merits inclusion in any listing of the nation's top business leaders of the late nineteenth and early twentieth century. Like most of the industrial capitalists of the age, Wood early displayed an entrepreneurial flair for turning a profit. Unlike most of those other giants, however, no biography of Wood has ever been written. His early life, aside from its business aspects, is almost unknown.

William Wood was the son of Portuguese parents who had emigrated from the Azores to Edgartown, Martha's Vineyard, Massachusetts. Little is known of his father's background except that he was born on October 6, 1827, on the island of Pico in the Azores. Not even his Portuguese surname can be authenticated. Various journalists have speculated that it was Jacinto, Madeira, or Silva.[1] Upon his arrival in America, he adopted the name William Jason Wood.[2] William Wood's mother, Amelia Christiana Madison, was also born on Pico, on December 25, 1838. She was of mixed English-Portuguese descent; her father, Charles Madison, was born in London, England and her mother, Christiana Amelia Dutra, was born in the Azores.[3]

The exact date of the arrival of William Wood's parents in the United States cannot be ascertained by available records. Apparently, neither William Jason Wood nor his wife ever became American citizens.[4] When or where they were married is also unknown. A search of marriage records for the decade of the 1850s in Edgartown, Vineyard Haven, and New Bedford, Massachusetts, revealed nothing. This suggests that they may have been married while still in the Azores.

How and why the couple left the island of Pico can only be surmised. As one of the nine small islands in the north Atlantic archipelago called the Azores, Pico consists mainly of the lofty 7,613-foot volcanic peak for which it is named. Farming and fishing have been the major occupation of its predominantly Portuguese population for over five centuries. In times of scarcity, often the only choice for those who desired a better life was to emigrate.

In the early decades of the nineteenth century, American whaling ships, which stopped in the Azores for supplies, provided the means for numerous young men to leave the islands. Since the men of Pico considered themselves the best sailors and fishermen in the islands, many of them signed on as crew members of the whalers.[5] In addition, some Azorean families made arrangements with the captains of the Yankee whalers to take their young sons aboard clandestinely. While these parents were eager to have their sons leave the archipelago to improve their economic status, they also wanted the lads to escape conscription.[6] During this period, the Azores were caught in the midst of the so-called Miguelist Wars, a bitter, prolonged struggle between feuding factions of the Portuguese royal family. Soldiers were needed throughout the Portuguese empire and the island's young men were routinely pressed into military service. When William Jason Wood reached the age of conscription, perhaps he also took the first opportunity available to avoid four years of colonial duty in Brazil, West Africa, or the Portuguese East Indies.

There is a legend that persists in Martha's Vineyard and New Bedford, Massachusetts, that Captain Henry Pease brought the frail, slender mariner

Pico, the Azores, birthplace of William Jason Wood and
Amelia Christiana Wood. (Courtesy of Carlos Barcelos)

from Pico in the 1850s. What gives remarkable support to this story is the known fact that on September 9, 1853, Captain Pease, commanding the 399-ton whaler, *Champion*, sailed out of Edgartown, Martha's Vineyard, on a lengthy whaling cruise. Thirty-three months later, on May 20, 1856, he returned to the port of Edgartown.[7] In all probability, the outward-bound *Champion* put into the Azores to take on supplies and to augment its crew. It is known that the *Champion* spoke to another vessel on September 16, 1853, at latitude 36° north and longitude 16° west, which is east-southeast of the Azores.[8] The legend has it that young Wood served as cook's assistant and was befriended by Captain Pease.

However William Jason Wood got to this country, upon his arrival in Edgartown he rented a fisherman's cottage on Pease's Point Way. It was to this cottage that the young mariner brought the eighteen-year-old Amelia

Christiana. When and how she left Pico is not known. Azorean mariners who left the islands aboard whalers often saved their wages and later sent for childhood sweethearts. Perhaps her father was able to underwrite her passage. A search of extant immigration records for the mid-1850s failed to reveal her point of entry into the United States.

On July 16, 1857, William Jason purchased the one-story cottage in Edgartown for $325.[9] Later he paid $75 for a piece of adjoining land. Although this seems a considerable sum for a recently arrived immigrant, it was not an unreasonable amount for a crew member of a successful whaler. The *Champion's* haul consisted of 1,857 barrels of oil and 16,700 pounds of whalebone.[10] Wood's share of the profits might have been $400, or perhaps Captain Pease lent him part of this sum. The latter possibility may have been essential if William also had paid for his wife's passage from Pico. Four children were born to the young couple during the five years they lived in this cottage. Their first child, Maria, was born in late 1856. On June 18, 1858, the first son, William, was born. A year later, Amelia Christiana gave birth to a second son, John M. A third son, Charles Jason, was born on April 6, 1861.

In that same year the Wood family relocated to New Bedford, Massachusetts, where they settled into another cramped cottage at 7 Jenney Street. Wood obtained a position as a steward on the steamer *Eagle's Wing*, which plied between Martha's Vineyard and New Bedford. His wife occasionally

Contemporary photograph of the birthplace of William M. Wood, Pease's Point Way, Edgartown, Martha's Vineyard, Massachusetts. (Photograph by Daniel F. Sullivan, Jr.)

The Commonwealth of Massachusetts
UNITED STATES OF AMERICA.
COPY OF RECORD OF BIRTH
TOWN of EDGARTOWN

I, the undersigned, hereby certify that I am clerk of the....Town....of....Edgartown....
that as such I have custody of the records of births required by law to be kept in my office; that among such records is one relating to the birth of

WILLIAM WOOD

and that the following is a true copy of so much of said record as relates to said birth, namely:

Date of Birth.... June 18, 1858

Place of Birth.... Edgartown

Name of Child.... William Wood

Sex.. Male   Color.... White

FATHER	MOTHER
Name.. Wm. Wood	Maiden Name.. Grace A. Wood
Residence.... Edgartown	Residence.... Edgartown
Place of Birth.... Pico, W.I.	Place of Birth.... Pico, W.I.
Occupation.... Mariner	

Date of Record........ January 17, 1859

SEAL

And I do hereby certify that the foregoing is a true copy from said records.
Witness my hand and seal of said Town of Edgartown
on this....4th....day of....June....19 80

Year.. 1858
Vol.. 1843-1876
Page.. 35
No.. 22

Anne L. Broome
Anne L. Broome   *Clerk*

Birth certificate of William M. Wood. It was common in the nineteenth century to refer to the Azores as the Western Islands. That his mother's maiden name is listed as Wood is puzzling.

worked as a scrubwoman on the vessel.[11] There are indications that Andrew G. Pierce, who was a wealthy New Bedford textile manufacturer and an agent for the company that owned the *Eagle's Wing*, may have befriended the struggling young family. Six years later the Woods would give the middle name Pierce to one of their sons, and nine years later Andrew Pierce would offer the young William Wood his first full-time job.

Between 1861 and 1870, the Wood couple had six additional children: Alfred, born in July 1864 (died in September 1864); Susan Pease (named for Captain Henry Pease?), born August 2, 1866; Otis Pierce, born November 29, 1867; Joseph, born sometime in 1868; Emma Rachael, born August 11, 1869; and Louise, born April 21, 1870 (died June 30, 1870). Charles Jason Wood died in 1867; Joseph also apparently died in childhood. Of the ten children, only Maria, William, John, Susan, Otis, and Emma would live to adulthood.

Cottages at 7 and 11 Jenney Street, New Bedford, Massachusetts. The Wood family lived at No. 7 from 1861 until 1876. They then moved to the adjacent larger house. (Photograph by Nicholas Whitman)

Like many immigrants, William Jason and Amelia Christiana Wood gave little thought to complying with all of the laws of their new homeland and were quite lax in recording the births and deaths of their children with the local authorities. Perhaps the mere struggle for existence occupied all their energy and attention. Whatever the reason, the children's births were not reported to the town officials until months—in one case, a year—after the event. Even then the information was not always complete. The birth certificate of Otis Pierce Wood, for example, reads "male child" and carries no name. Baptismal records are also incomplete. Otis Pierce's baptismal certificate gives his name as Antone and lists December 24, 1867, as date of birth. That the parents were practicing Roman Catholics seems doubtful, since they only had four of the ten children baptized, usually several years after birth. Antone (Otis Pierce), Christiana (Emma Rachael), Charles (Charles Jason), and Joseph were christened between 1863 and 1870.[12] The fact that two of these four children appear to have both English/American and Portuguese names, may be due to Roman Catholic officials insisting that Otis Pierce and Emma were not acceptable as baptismal names.

It was apparently a constant struggle for William Jason Wood to make ends meet. He moved from one menial job to another. He was variously a cobbler, a fisherman, a steward, an eating saloon keeper, a city watchman, a shipyard worker, and a day laborer. In 1864 William Jason, in the company of John Adams Pease, brother of Captain Henry Pease, went to Chelsea to find work as a shipbuilder.[13] It was there that Alfred and Susan Pease Wood were born. Apparently, Mrs. Wood accompanied her husband to Chelsea while the older children continued to live at 7 Jenney Street in New Bedford. Maria, William, and John were students at the Cannonville Grammar School in New Bedford during these years. Who took care of the children while the parents were living in Chelsea is not known.

In a 1923 interview, William Wood remarked: "As my father was away most of the time . . . I saw very little of him. Under the circumstances he could not mean much in my life. My mother was everything. Always gentle, sweet and loving . . . A woman of genuine refinement and a mother of never-failing goodness and kindness. . . ."[14] Elsewhere, Amelia Christiana Wood is described as "fragile and delicate in appearance as Vista Alegre [a fine Portuguese porcelain noted for its exceptional whiteness and its durability] porcelain and apparently as durable."[15] Between 1856 and the end of 1870, she bore William Jason Wood ten children and saw at least three of them, as well as her husband, die.

On August 21, 1870, William Jason Wood died of consumption. He was buried in the Catholic Burial Grounds of St. Mary's Church in New Bedford. The death of the father precipitated a family crisis. William, barely twelve, had graduated from Cannonville Grammar School in 1868 and was a student at New Bedford High School. He was forced to leave school and seek employment to help support his working mother and younger siblings, who ranged in age from one to four. In later years William Madison Wood (he had added the middle name while still in his teens) reminisced, "When my father died, I started to work. That was where my good fortune began."[16]

As a matter of fact, young William Wood was already working at the time of his father's death. He had a part-time summer job as a cash boy in George M. Eddy's drygoods store in New Bedford. The Quaker merchant paid the lad a weekly wage of $1.25.[17]

At the time of William Wood's death in 1926, much was written about his achievements during his school years. As with many a tale from the past, there is little documentation to support these press accounts. The records of the Cannonville School, located less than a mile from Jenney Street, were accidentally destroyed some years ago. The ten-year-old William entered New Bedford High School in September 1868, younger by more than a year than his classmates. His high school records indicate little to suggest his later

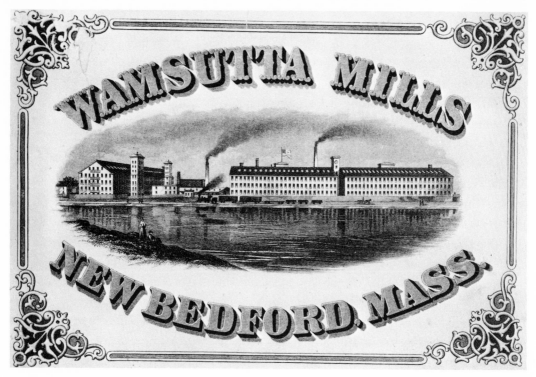

Cloth label of the Wamsutta Mills, New Bedford, Massachusetts. It was in these cotton mills that William Wood gained his first experience in textile manufacturing. (Courtesy of Merrimack Valley Textile Museum)

success.[18] He ranked fifty-second in a class of fifty-four at the end of his third and final term in July of 1870. On a scale of 1 to 10, his grades were Latin 5.9, French 7.8, Philosophy 7.4, Diction 7, and Composition 8. His last recorded grade for "Deportment" in November 1869 was 10, which suggests he was a well-behaved youngster. That "he excelled in Greek and kept a diary in German" as some of his obituaries reported would appear the fancy of over-eager journalists. There is no record of his enrollment in either Greek or German language classes. Perhaps his parents thought him "an early achiever," when they entered the youth in high school in 1868. Over the years William Wood would prove their hopes more than well founded. But the year was 1870 and the young boy, who loved to play marbles, was faced with finding a job that would help support his family.[19]

William apparently did not have to look very long, for Andrew G. Pierce, treasurer of the Wamsutta Cotton Mills of New Bedford, made him an office boy in the firm's counting room at a salary of four dollars a week. While such a salary may be minimal by today's standards, it was considerably more than boys of his age normally earned at that time. Wood would always remember his first full-time job in Pierce's office on the second floor of the Merchants

28

National Bank on North Water Street. Forty-seven years later, when he was a wealthy man, he purchased the building for sentimental reasons.[20]

The New Bedford of Wood's youth was undergoing a social and economic metamorphosis. It had earned both fame and fortune as a whaling port in the late eighteenth and early nineteenth centuries. Herman Melville made it the home port of Captain Ahab in his classic novel *Moby Dick* (1851). By the time William Jason Wood arrived in America, the great herds of sperm whales had been depleted by overfishing. Furthermore, Edwin Drake's discovery of petroleum in the rich oil fields of western Pennsylvania in 1859 heralded the birth of the kerosene age of illumination and dealt a death blow to the already ailing whale oil industry. It was in these years that the city of New Bedford found a new source of wealth and work—the cotton textile industry. Although William Madison Wood's mariner father had failed to achieve either fame or fortune in this southern coastal city of Massachusetts, here the son would embark upon his remarkable career.

In his later life, William Wood always called New Bedford "my home."

Merchants National Bank Building, New Bedford, Massachusetts. Andrew G. Pierce had his office here in the early 1870s, when he hired Wood as an office boy. In 1918, Wood purchased the building "for sentimental reasons." (Photograph by Stephen F. Adams, circa 1872. Courtesy of Old Dartmouth Historical Society Whaling Museum, New Bedford, Massachusetts)

Most of his first twenty-two years were spent there. Wood later recalled: "I was mighty lucky in getting into such an office, for there I met the leading citizens of the town. The officers and directors of the Wamsutta Mills were exceptional men. . . . I have never met their superior in all my experience since then. . . ."[21]

Wood's assignments as office boy occasionally took him down to the cotton mills themselves, where his inquisitive mind absorbed the details of the production process. "I asked questions of everybody—superintendents, foremen, operators. . . . From the very beginning, I was curious about the cost of things. . . ."[22] He would look at two different pieces of cloth, and ponder "how much of the general mill costs each one bore." Out of his youthful fascination with production costs would eventually emerge a decimal point cost system which John D. Rockefeller might have admired.

After three years as an office boy, still at four dollars a week, he asked to be transferred to the manufacturing department of the Wamsutta concern. Although Wood was never a mill operative, he kept "bell time" during the six-day workweek. That is, when the factory bell sounded at 6:10 A.M., he started to work. He worked until the bell sounded at 6:00 P.M., with thirty minutes off for lunch. His exact duties in the cotton mill are not known.

Details of the young man's family and social life during these years are almost unknown. Thanks to the New Bedford Free Public Library, Wood continued to study on his own. He was especially interested in mathematics. Despite his long work day, he also taught himself to play the violin. To lessen family financial straits, his younger brothers John and Otis evidently struck out on their own.[23] His sisters may have also worked to supplement William's salary.

In 1876 young Wood turned eighteen and decided to see something of the world beyond New Bedford. That year was also the nation's one-hundredth birthday, and the great Philadelphia Centennial was in progress. Wood talked the captain of a local schooner into taking him on the next scheduled run to Philadelphia. "The trip took six days and I was seasick five of them!"[24] The youth was sufficiently impressed with the City of Brotherly Love and the 450-acre exhibit in Fairmont Park to stay for six months. He marveled at the striking architecture of Independence Hall, and he was impressed by the tree-lined avenues and stately homes of the city.

To support himself during his stay, Wood later recounted, he secured employment in the office of a dockside coal company at the now familiar four dollars a week wage. After paying his room and board, he had fifty cents left for spending money. Another source suggests that in addition, his old mentor,

Andrew G. Pierce, secured a post in a Philadelphia bank for the young Wood, and it was there that he got his first taste of the intricate world of the stock exchange.[25]

By early winter 1876, Wood had grown homesick for his mother and sisters and had returned to New Bedford. Here he obtained a position with the banking house of J. A. Beauvais & Company, where one of his tasks was to keep the books of the firm of James B. Ward and Company, whaling merchants. For more than twenty-three years Mr. Beauvais had been the only person to meticulously enter information upon the ledgers, journals, and cash books of the concern. Wood in later years joked, "I was the first man to make blots and errors and scratches upon the books."[26] Still he was learning the business and becoming a skilled accountant. His wages at the bank were also four dollars a week. Almost half a century later, Wood wryly reminisced, "I thought I would never get away from that four-dollar salary."[27]

The four-dollar-a-week positions did end, however. In 1877 the New Bedford and Fall River Railroad offered him a position at forty dollars a month. His accounting and banking experiences were now paying off for him. Nevertheless, the manufacture of textiles was his main interest, and in 1880 he left New Bedford for the Fall River cotton mills. For the next six years he worked as paymaster and assistant to Otis M. Pierce, son of his former employer. He was also assistant to Edward L. Anthony, treasurer of the Border City Mill. For the remainder of his business career, Wood would be associated with the textile industry.

By 1886, Wood was earning a salary of $1,400 a year. His youthful habit of asking questions of everyone from mill operative to agent stayed with him. As he grew older and more knowledgeable about the intricacies of the textile world, his questions grew sharper and more perceptive. His reputation as a dynamic, creative young man grew apace. In late 1886, Wood and several business friends journeyed to Providence, Rhode Island, to solicit subscriptions for a cotton mill, which they planned to build in Fall River. Wood was to be general manager of the proposed plant.[28] Wood's career plans abruptly changed, however, and he would shortly relocate to Lawrence, Massachusetts.

To understand how this change came about, it is necessary to look at the history of Lawrence. The town had been chartered by the General Court of Massachusetts in 1847 and named in honor of Abbott Lawrence. Two years earlier, a group of Boston merchants, including Abbott Lawrence, had formed the Essex Company with the intention of harnessing the water power of the Merrimack River at this site for cotton and woolen textile factories. Along with the factories, they built a model town with parks and supervised boarding houses to entice the daughters of New England farm families to work in their mills. At first, the Boston Brahmins kept a careful, paternal watch over their creation. Within a few years, however, the labor shortage that had mandated such solicitous plans ended, and a new source of cheap labor appeared. The town soon lost its half-rural character and turned into a city of immigrants.[29]

First, there was a trickle of English, Scots, and Germans. Then came a veritable tidal wave of Irish fleeing the horrors of the potato famine of the late 1840s. In 1848, Lawrence had a population of nearly 6,000. "Of that number, 3,750 were of native birth; 2,139 were natives of Ireland; there were one German, one Italian, three Frenchmen, two Welshmen, nine natives of Scotland, 28 people of English birth and 16 negroes...."[30] By 1875 there were 8,000 Irish in a population of 35,000. Also by that date, French Canadians, fleeing the harsh rural poverty of Quebec, had flooded into the city. Ten years later in 1885, Lawrence had a population of 38,862, of whom 43.99 percent were foreign born. Throughout the 1880s and 1890s, still more immigrants arrived. Italians, Lithuanians, Poles, Syrians, and Jews inundated the city in

Bird's-eye drawing of Lawrence, Massachusetts, 1876.
(Courtesy of Merrimack Valley Textile Museum)

AYER'S SARSAPARILLA
CURED
SCROFULA, DYSPEPSIA
BONES, CATARRH
BOILS, Rheumatism
HUMORS, DEBILITY
TETTER, All Disorders or the
ECZEMA, BLOOD.

AYER'S SARSAPARILLA
The DEACON: "Land sake Liza, the very
sight of that bottle makes me feel like another man"

AYER'S SARSAPARILLA IS A COMPOUND CONCENTRATED EXTRACT—
THE STRONGEST, BEST, CHEAPEST BLOOD MEDICINE.

M IND **W**HILE THE DEACON is explaining to 'Liza the merits of AYER'S SARSA-PARILLA, *bear in mind* that it is not a mixture of cheap or dangerous drugs, but a **highly concentrated extract** of the genuine **Honduras Sarsaparilla** and other choice medicinal roots, alterative, diuretic, and tonic; the same being united with the **Iodides of Potassium** and **Iron**, forming by far the most economical, safe, and reliable blood-purifying medicine ever offered to the public.

If there is a lurking taint of Scrofula about you, AYER'S SARSAPARILLA will expel it from your system.

For the cure of lassitude, debility, and all disorders peculiar to the Spring, it has proved to be the best remedy ever devised.

If your blood is impure, cleanse it without delay by the use of AYER'S SARSAPARILLA.

PREPARED BY

Dr. J. C. AYER & CO., Lowell, Mass.

FOR SALE BY

"THE DEACON." — A fine Chromo-Lithograph (7 x 13 inches, in "Statuette" style) of this original and popular subject, will be sent, post-paid, to any address, with a set of our elegant Album Cards, on receipt of 10 cents in cash or postage stamps. Address

Dr. J. C. AYER & CO., Lowell, Mass.

J. C. Ayer and Company Trade Card (front and back).
(Courtesy of Clarisse Poirier)

search of employment in the great mill complex. Abbott Lawrence's model town had, by the end of the century, evolved into a teeming conglomeration of sprawling slums and bustling, noisy factories wherein foreign languages were heard more often than English.

Onto this scene in 1885 stepped Frederick Ayer of Lowell, Massachusetts, one of New England's wealthiest men. Born in Ledyard, Connecticut, on December 8, 1822, Ayer was descended from the earliest settlers of New England. In the 1840s, he had entered the mercantile business in Syracuse, New York. He had continued in this business under a partnership with Dennis McCarthy (McCarthy & Ayer) until 1855. In that year, he had joined his brother, Dr. James C. Ayer, in the management of the prospering J. C. Ayer Company of Lowell, which specialized in the manufacture and sale of cherry pectoral, sarsaparilla, ague cure, hair restorer, and other patent medicines. It also published the popular Ayer Almanac, which was replete with glowing accounts of the wonders of Ayer's Proprietary Medicines.[31] The Ayer Almanac was a phenomenon in and of itself. The firm's print shop ran off 16,000,000 copies a year in twenty-one languages. Indeed, in one year the total may have soared over 25,000,000 copies. The J. C. Ayer Company's modest slogan for its publication was, "Second only to the Bible in circulation—is Ayer's Almanac."

By the 1860s both brothers were wealthy entrepreneurs with ample capital to invest in other attractive business enterprises. In 1871 they purchased controlling interest in several Lowell cotton concerns and consolidated them under the name of the Tremont and Suffolk Mills. This was not the first venture into textile manufacturing for James C. Ayer. Early in the 1850s, before Frederick joined the firm, the older brother had invested heavily in the Bay State Mills of Lawrence. In the financial panic of 1857, the mills had failed. James Ayer had lost $2,000,000 in the disaster.[32]

Some years later, the buildings of the defunct Bay State Mills (with several newer structures added) were opened for business as the Washington Mills, a woolen and cotton producing corporation. Frederick Ayer invested heavily in the concern. In June 1885 the Washington Mills went into bankruptcy and the property was put up for auction. Frederick Ayer was convinced that the firm's collapse had been engineered by Harding, Colby & Company, the commission selling-house that handled the output of the Washington Mills. When he attended the auction, his suspicions seemed to be confirmed. There was only one bidder—Harding, Colby & Company. Furious at what he felt was about to happen, he outbid them and bought the mill complex for a mere $328,000. He tore down the old, narrow mills (some of them nine stories tall) and sold the machinery for a sum equal to his purchase price. Ayer built in their stead a new mill complex equipped with the most modern American and English machinery.[33]

The enterprise was costly, and Ayer as the major stockholder poured almost $2,000,000 into the construction of the Washington Mills Company. To run the new woolen and cotton mills, he hired Thomas Sampson, a textile manufacturer from Rhode Island, as manager. The latter's salary was $25,000 a year. By late 1886 the firm was losing money at such a rate that not even one of New England's richest tycoons could long afford to underwrite such a losing proposition. These costly ventures into the textile industry by both Ayer brothers suggest that they were ill-equipped and ill-advised to embark upon such high-priced investments. Their phenomenal success in the field of patent medicine was of no help in the manufacture of cloth. What they needed were capable men to handle the day-to-day operations of their mills, which made up one of the largest textile concerns of its time. Sampson was qualified, but his prior experience had been with much smaller woolen opera-

34

Frederick Ayer (1822–1918), owner of the Washington Mills, Lawrence, Massachusetts. He served as president of the American Woolen Company from 1899 to 1905. (*Bulletin*, National Association of Wool Manufacturers, 1918)

tions. The task before him was too big to handle by himself. In desperation, Sampson looked about for an experienced man to head the cotton-manufacturing department of the Washington Mills. He met Wood in Providence when the latter was soliciting subscriptions for his proposed cotton mill. Sampson offered the young man a salary of $1,800 a year. Wood accepted.[34]

By Christmas, 1886, William Wood had found lodgings at 37 Jackson Street in Lawrence and was busy trying to stop the disastrous drain on Ayer's investment. A short time later, Wood was thunderstruck to learn that the board of directors had voted to abolish the cotton department and devote the plant's entire resources to wool manufacturing. He asked Sampson to put him in charge of woolen production. "If I was competent to handle the cotton manufacturing, I'm competent to make good in wool,"[35] he asserted. While the logic of this boast does not stand close examination, Sampson nonetheless gave him the position. Sampson soon became dissatisfied, however, and told Wood that he would have to let him go. The twenty-nine-year-old Wood was stunned. Never had he been discharged from a position. Worse still, Sampson suggested that Wood was incompetent. Wood later recounted how he left the agent's office and walked aimlessly about the streets of Lawrence. Seldom had his life looked so dark as it did that wintery day. He dreaded the prospect of returning to New Bedford or Fall River "a failure." The Washington Mills were modern and up-to-date. Why wasn't the company making money? These and other thoughts went through his mind as he stared at the ice-clogged Merrimack River. An idea came to him. He raced back to Sampson's desk and asked to be appointed salesman for the Washington Mills Company. At that time, yarns were not sold by company salesmen; manufacturers either sat back and waited for customers to come to them or, more commonly, utilized the services of selling houses. Sampson and Ayer apparently liked the innovative suggestion, and they agreed to Wood's request for a salary of $2,500 a year. That very night Wood packed his valise and headed out of the city aboard a Boston and Maine train.

His first six weeks on the road must have been disappointing. After visiting scores of buyers in New York, Boston, Philadelphia, and elsewhere, he failed to secure a single order. Lesser men might have been discouraged, but not William Wood. He knew that the various yarns of the Washington Mills Company were the equal of, if not superior to, the yarns of competing firms. Indeed, their blue flannel coating was without equal. Wood persevered; he shaved prices, under-bid competitors, and proved to be an uncanny salesman. By the end of 1887, he had sold $2,000,000 worth of woolen goods, and the Washington Mills took on new life.[36]

Frederick Ayer, meanwhile, had become dissatisfied with Sampson's management of the company and had replaced him with Francis H. Jealous of Lawrence. In 1889, Ayer called Wood back to Lawrence and put him in charge of the mills as well as the selling.[37] His salary was now $25,000 a year. This was a princely sum compared to the four dollars a week salary he had been earning just thirteen years before.

While the reorganized firm showed a modest profit, its refusal to deal with the woolen selling, or commission, houses had created a credit problem of

Washington Mills, Lawrence, Massachusetts, circa 1910.
(Courtesy of Merrimack Valley Textile Museum)

serious dimensions. Like the vast majority of textile manufacturing firms, the Washington Mills did not have sufficient working capital to carry on its everyday business without borrowing money. Normally the needed funds were obtained from banks by giving them the firm's note endorsed by the commission house. Without such an endorsement, banks refused to advance the necessary monies. Ayer, accordingly, was obliged to advance as much as $6,000,000 of his own family fortune to the Washington Mills. Such underwriting could not long continue, as Ayer wrote to his son James in October of 1889.

> ... Wish you would talk with Wood about our credit system. We can't afford to furnish all Jerusalem capital to fail on. To the failures reported yesterday add Anspach $2,514.00, and others less important and you will see—if continued— we must follow their example. J. C. Ayer Co. has not lost as much by failures in ten years. These three would pay for all the dinamo's [sic] and new twisters and machinery that Wood is crying for, and I don't dare to order.[38]

Wood, eager to improve the efficiency of the Washington Mills, evidently was dunning his superior for still additional money for new plant equipment. Perhaps the reason Ayer did not criticize his employee directly was that, by this time, Wood was more than Ayer's only hope for putting the Washington Mills on a paying basis—he was also his son-in-law.

Ellen Wheaton Ayer, aged twenty-nine, and William Madison Wood, aged thirty, were married on Thursday afternoon, November 21, 1888, in the drawing room of the Ayer mansion on Pawtucket Street in Lowell. The Reverend Julian K. Smyth, pastor of the New Jerusalem Church in Roxbury, performed the private, simple Swedenborgian ceremony. Ellen was the eldest of Frederick Ayer's children by his first wife, Cornelia Wheaton (1858–1878). In her teens she had attended a fashionable French "young ladies" school, Les Ruches, in Fontainbleau, some twenty miles southeast of Paris. Upon her return to the United States, she had enrolled at Radcliffe College.[39] Wood probably first met her at one of Ayer's frequent Sunday dinner parties in early 1888. Ellen, a petite, vivacious woman and a graceful dancer, loved music, painting, and literature. She spoke French and was widely traveled. As a daughter of one of New England's wealthiest families, she must have had numerous suitors before meeting Wood.

The marriage of this aristocratic young lady to the son of Portuguese immigrants must have raised eyebrows in Massachusetts society. Her ancestors had settled in Connecticut in the eighteenth century; Wood's parents had come from the Azores only a quarter-century before the wedding. Ellen's brothers were Harvard graduates; Wood had never finished high school. Her world was one of culture and refinement; his, thus far, had been one of work.

After their honeymoon, the young couple settled into a spacious residence in Winchester, Massachusetts. While Ellen was busy decorating their new home and hiring a staff of servants, William returned to work. He was determined to make the Washington Mills a profitable undertaking for both his father-in-law and himself.

Wood's path would not be an easy one, for the decade of the 1890s proved to be a rocky road not only for the textile industry but for the nation's economy as a whole. "Economic activity in the United States had, by these years reached a new stage of interdependence whereby a weakness in any major part of the system unavoidably enfeebled the rest."[40] The portrayal of this decade of American history as the "gay" or "naughty nineties" is misleading. Except for the few exciting months of the Chicago World's Fair in the summer of 1893, there was little gaiety in the period. As for naughtiness, that was limited to a handful of New York nouveaux riches. In June 1893 the nation's stock market crashed. In the wake of this financial debacle, 600 banks closed, 15,000 commercial houses failed, and 74 railroads went into receivership. There followed five years of deep depression, which "pushed agriculture to its lowest depth [and] demoralized industry and transportation. . . ."[41]

The business stagnation that characterized these five dreary years of depression was particularly sharp in the textile industry. Cancelled orders, wage reductions, lay-offs, cutbacks in production, and diminished profits were widespread. The woolen manufacturers created some of their own worst problems. Competition was traditionally cutthroat, but the depression brought out more atavistic tendencies in many owners. Darwin's "law of the jungle" and "survival of the fittest" seemed to rule most business dealings. In addition, a large number of the textile mills were equipped with antiquated machinery and staffed by inefficient management. As one observer of the period stated:

> The industry was demoralized by practices generally condemned, but which individuals seemed unable to abolish or appreciably to check. . . . Kindred abuses had been carried further in the marketing of wool manufactures than in any other line of goods, and as they increased, manufacturers despaired of a remedy and the markets, it was said, were in the hands of the buyers to do with pretty much as they pleased.[42]

Cancellation of orders had become so chronic that a contract had ceased to have any validity. On top of these problems, the industry was suffering from the effects of the Wilson-Gorman Tariff of 1894. The Democratic Congress had put woolen cloth on the free list, and cheap foreign cloth (particularly from England and the continent) was dumped onto the domestic market. Many of the nation's woolen firms faced economic ruin.

The Washington Mills were caught in the midst of this turmoil. For Wood, who had been named treasurer in 1895, it was vital that he stem the mill's repeated yearly deficits. There was a saying in the textile industry in those years that any establishment that owed a million dollars was irretrievably lost. The Washington Mills had a debt of $3,000,000. The cause looked hopeless to everyone save Wood.

The major problem plaguing the firm, as well as most other woolen textile concerns, was the high cost of labor per unit of production. A high turnover in the labor force compounded this liability. Wood instituted a bonus system for higher production. The speedup in production did not make him popular with mill operatives, but the Washington Mills soon boasted of a stable work force. More importantly, in Wood's thinking, this measure added considerably to plant production.

The treasurer insisted upon meticulous cost accounting reports from every branch of the firm. Bookkeepers supplied him with weekly cost analysis summaries, something which was unheard of elsewhere in the industry. Wood demanded as much of his machinery as of his employees. Once he discovered a more efficient piece of machinery, be it a loom or twister or spindle, he ordered its purchase and installation. While Ayer continued as president, it was his son-in-law who ran the Washington Mills.

Wood kept a careful eye on every official in the company. Rapid promotions went to the most able and innovative. He personally trained those assistants who supervised the day-to-day operations of the large concern. He sent his salesmen scurrying to garment buyers in order to meet their weekly sales quotas. Wood drove himself and those who worked for him. He moved a cot into his office and usually put in a sixteen- or seventeen-hour workday.[43]

The changes that Wood instituted were considered so unorthodox that other mill owners predicted disaster. One of his fellow mill directors in Lawrence wrote:

> This young man's notions are certain to wreck him and everybody connected with him. He imagines that he can keep, separately, the cost of each process in manufacturing. The real trouble with the Washington Mills is their great size. They are far too big to be operated profitably. In a factory of that size you can't keep any reliable costs, and you can't get the right organization.[44]

Wood persisted in pressing for increased efficiency, and his father-in-law stood by him.

In 1897 the Republican Congress that had come into power with the election of President William McKinley repealed the Wilson-Gorman legislation and enacted the Dingley Tariff, which restored protection of sorts to the nation's woolen manufacturers. By then, however, "New England was like the shores of the ocean after a mighty storm. The wrecks of the woolen mills were strewn all over it."[45] Nevertheless, the Washington Mills not only succeeded in riding out the storm, in 1898 they showed a profit.

Around this time Wood began toying with a more grandiose plan. If, by his innovative measures, he could put the deficit-producing Washington Mills in the black, why couldn't the same be done with a number of woolen and worsted mills?[46] The idea intrigued him. He envisioned combining them into a single, strong, well-financed, and ably-managed concern.

The practice of business consolidation had grown dramatically during the 1890s. Neither state laws nor the Sherman Anti-trust Act of 1890 could arrest the movement toward consolidation. Indeed, in the three years from 1898 to 1900, 149 combinations were effected nation-wide with a total capitalization of $3,784,000,000. "Only in these final years of the century did consolidation really begin to dominate American industry. Even so, only a third of the combinations organized in the nineties could be called 'trusts' in the popular sense—that is, consolidations large enough to monopolize an industry."[47] The trend toward such consolidations began in the railroad, banking, steel, and sugar industries, although the "bigger is better" belief quickly spread to other fields. The inducements were attractive. Competition would be lessened, good prices assured, and a large working capital made available through the sale of stock. Best of all, some sort of stability would be established. At least, that was what a growing number of entrepreneurs believed.

In this sense, Wood's idea was not novel. Yet the shipwrecked woolen manufacturers to whom he presented the plan thought it a radical suggestion. "Gentlemen, would you like to get aboard?" he asked. "Absurd" was the general reply. "Impossible," "wild idea" were the terms he constantly encountered. They argued that such an undertaking could never succeed. Wood, however, was a man of determination and vision who saw many desirable possibilities in such a woolen combination. He won his father-in-law's backing, and Frederick Ayer carried considerable weight in the textile world. Finally, after a tremendous struggle against hostile criticism and opposition, Wood convinced the owners of seven other mills to join with the Washington Mills. "Such an organization would be good for the industry, good for labor, for mill conditions and for the public," he argued.[48] Nearly all of the mills which entered into the combination had been in bankruptcy or in some serious financial plight. It looked like a risky venture at best.

Wood later recounted how he called in the other mill owners. One by one he questioned them. "What is your cost system?" was his first question. One of the men produced a paper bag covered with a maze of illegible figures. Another had a few indecipherable figures on the flyleaf of a ledger.[49] This sort of slipshod cost system had been partially responsible for the plight in which many of the mill owners found themselves. Wood's combination would put an end to such practices.

Experts had long argued that a trust or monopoly in the woolen industry was impossible.

> Because . . . the diversity of woolen products was so great, the influence of fashions upon the demand for goods was so decisive, and the opportunity for individual skill and enterprise was so broad, that a shrewd manufacturer could always invade any field he desired, regardless of the monopolistic competition, by creating a specialty that appealed to the public taste.[50]

Such reasons were cogent, and Wood's creation was not a monopoly. His consolidation of the eight firms into one would face the competition of 500 other woolen manufacturers in New England alone. Even so, news of the merger sent mild shock waves throughout the woolen manufacturing states.[51]

To handle the legal details of this first multi-million dollar woolen merger, Wood turned to the "father of trusts," Charles R. Flint. This financier and speculator had earlier (1892) brought about the formation of the giant United States Rubber Company. Flint was "one of the marrying parsons of big business. . . . His chief personal services seem to have been discovering possible consolidations, getting together the persons concerned, and suggesting terms and compromises."[52] In the same year that he brought about Wood's merger, Flint also organized the Sloss Sheffield Company, the American Chicle Company, and the United States Bobbin & Shuttle Company.

On February 28, 1899, the American Woolen Company held its first organizational meeting in the Waldorf-Astoria hotel in New York City. On March 29 the firm was incorporated under the laws of New Jersey. The financial side of Wood's creation was noteworthy in at least one respect: it was carried out without the issue of bonds. The firm was authorized to issue $25,000,000 of preferred stock and $40,000,000 of common stock. Of these amounts $20,000,000 of preferred and $29,500,000 of common were issued at once.

> The greater portion of the common stock was used in the purchase of the mills, owners taking 50 percent in cash and 50 percent in common stock of the new company; but $16,000,000 of the preferred and $8,000,000 of the common stock were sold to provide cash for the purchase of the mills and to secure working capital for the concern.[53]

Common-stock holders were not guaranteed a definite dividend rate, but they could vote at shareholders' meetings in proportion to their holdings. Owners of preferred stock received dividends before any dividends could be paid to holders of common stock. Additionally, the former had preference in the distribution of assets.

Apparently there was a considerable amount of over-capitalization or "watering" as Wall Streeters termed it. The census of 1899 indicates the average capitalization for all mills producing woolen and worsted goods as $4,204 per loom. For the American Woolen Company, upon its formation, the average capitalization for each of its 5,400 looms was approximately $9,150. "Accordingly, though the Company itself subsequently placed the value of its original plants at $40,000,000, a more reasonable estimate would probably have halved that figure. . . ."[54]

Included in the original merger were four Massachusetts firms: the Washington Mills of Lawrence, the Fitchburg Worsted Company and the Beoli Company of Fitchburg, and the Saranac Worsted Mills of Blackstone; three Rhode Island firms: the National & Providence Worsted Mills, the Valley Worsted Mills, and the Riverside Worsted Mills, all of Providence; and one New York firm: the Fulton Worsted Mills of Fulton, New York. At the time of the combination, the value of the eight mills was appraised at $12,000,000.

Their certified earnings for the five years preceding the merger were $2,593,000. The Washington Mills were the oldest (established in 1858), the largest, and the most efficient of the group. The products of the merged units included men's clothing, women's cloakings and dress goods, fancy cashmeres, worsteds, French-spun worsted yarns, and ordinary worsted yarns.

Within ten minutes after the corporation papers were executed at the Waldorf-Astoria meeting, $10,000,000 of the preferred stock had been subscribed. Ayer was the largest single investor. Wood's share of stock is not known, but it must have been considerable.[55] After all, he was the one who had conceived the merger, and he was the one who would be responsible for making a success of the venture. Ayer was named president and William Wood treasurer. April 17, 1899, was the first day of business for the new company. Years later, Frederick Ayer wrote:

> Henry Lee Higginson and other prominent businessmen said it was too complicated ever to succeed. Higginson was so confident in his prophecy that his company [Lee, Higginson & Company] would not handle the stock of the Woolen Company. The company had $5,000,000 of its preferred stock in its treasury, of which Higginson knew, and after we had been running about two years he came to me and said: "Why don't you put out that $5,000,000 of preferred stock? It will save your borrowing just so much money." I said: "Because you and men like you haven't the confidence to distribute it." "Oh well," he said, "I used to think the concern would never succeed, but Wood has made it a success and that settles that question."[56]

Barely forty-one years of age in 1899, William Madison Wood stood poised and ready to move into the twentieth century.

21 Fairfield Street (corner of Commonwealth Avenue) Boston, Massachusetts.
The Wood family maintained a residence here from the 1890s until the 1920s.
(Photograph by Phillip Naylor)

Arden, the Andover, Massachusetts estate of William M. Wood. (Author's collection)

CHAPTER III

Paterfamilias

Aside from the sketchy details of William Wood's early life in New Bedford, Massachusetts, next to nothing is known of his personal life in the years between his leaving school in 1870 and late 1888, when he married. That he was a "workaholic" seems obvious. By the late 1890s, however, it is known that he was a family man and to his spouse and children he gave generously of his love and attention. Wood probably spent Christmas, 1899 in the company of his growing family. By this date, Ellen Ayer Wood had borne him four children: two sons and two daughters. Rosalind, the eldest, was born in Winchester on August 17, 1889. William Madison Wood, Jr. was born on January 26, 1892, Cornelius Ayer Wood on October 9, 1893, and Irene, the youngest, on December 29, 1894. The latter three children were born in Andover.

In these years the Wood family had grown dissatisfied with the Winchester residence and now divided its time between their Boston home, a five-story, brick structure at 21 Fairfield Street in the Back Bay, and their rural estate, which they called Arden, in Andover. The Boston residence had been built in 1880 for G. P. King. The architect, W. Whitney Lewis, had modeled the structure on H. H. Richardson's rectory of Trinity Church in Boston. Although the definitive study *The Houses of Boston's Back Bay* dismisses Lewis' creation as "complete artistic indigestion," the Wood family loved the spacious mansion.[1] It stood at the corner of Farfield Street and Common-wealth Avenue and was but a few steps from the Boston Museum of Fine Arts and the Boston Public Library. Within a short carriage ride was the ornate home of Grandfather Ayer at 395 Commonwealth Avenue. The Ayer mansion was designed and built by the architect A. J. Manning in 1899, when the elder Ayer was seventy-seven years of age.[2] Mrs. Wood and the children frequently visited there on Sundays.

For the Woods, and especially for the children, Arden was their favorite home. Wood had wanted a house close to Lawrence and the Washington Mills, and he found it in Andover. The twenty-room, Carpenter Gothic resi-dence had been built in 1847 for John Dove, a partner in the Smith & Dove flax manufacturing firm of Frye Village.[3] Jacob Chickering of Andover had erected the rambling frame structure atop a gentle hill, which nestled at the edge of a fifty-acre estate of sweeping lawns and meadows.

After William Wood purchased the property in 1891, he began a series of enlargements that continued for the next fifteen years. Wood added to the house and improved the grounds—a new wing here, a tennis court there, several miles of roadway. He planted trees, erected hen houses, enlarged the stables, constructed a porte-cochère at the main entrance of the residence, and, more than likely, added the elaborate gingerbread carving to the ridge roof. He also acquired an additional ten acres along the edge of the original estate.

Wood thoroughly enjoyed dabbling in architecture not only at Arden but at residences which he later built on Cuttyhunk Island in Buzzard's Bay, Massachusetts, and in Palm Beach, Florida. Indeed, Wood sometimes seemed to have almost a compulsion to build. His greatest architectural experiment would be his model community, Shawsheen Village, which he would erect on the site of Frye Village in the early twentieth century.

Rosalind, the eldest of the Wood children, later recalled: "Arden was our love and joy! There was no place on earth so delightful, or beautiful."[4] The great white house with green shutters, irregular chimneys, and the ginger-bread carving, which the children called "icicles," was surmounted by a tower-ing roof. In the center of the roof was a cupola to delight the heart of any adventurous child. Inside the house an elaborately carved mahogany grand staircase with its polished railing was a challenge to the two boys, who slid down it when Mother was not about.

Some two hundred yards north of the residence was a large pond. Here the children and their friends came for swimming and boating in the summer and for ice-skating in the winter. On the western edge of the pond stood a three-story shingled structure, which had originally been part of the Poor Wagon Manufacturing Company of Frye Village. This building was used by the Wood family for dances, live theatre, and gala celebrations on the Fourth of July. They called it The Casino.

The children loved pets and there was always a collection of dogs, cats, rabbits, ducks, Hereford calves, ponies, and donkeys wandering about the grounds. Barns and stables and a Gothic greenhouse for Mrs. Wood's flowers were filled with all sorts of hidden corners, which made the game of hide-and-seek such fun for the children. On the north side of the residence stood a lovely formal garden trimmed with cedar hedges.

"In the early 1900s domestic help was readily obtainable. The going wage for the best of them was $1.00 per day," Cornelius Wood later wrote.[5] There were a cook, maids, gardeners, coachmen, and, later, chauffeurs. A series of governesses cared for the children until they were ready to go off to boarding school.

In their early years, the children did not see much of their father. He was off to his Boston office or to one of the Lawrence mills before they awakened. Yet their childhood memories of him are pleasant ones. His evening home-coming was always an opportunity for games and story-telling. Sometimes on a winter evening, he would drop to all fours inside the front door, wrap his fur coat about himself, and allow the children to pound him with rolled magazines as he pretended to be a bear.[6] Sunday was the best day of the week for the youngsters, for it was the only day that they had their father all to themselves. There was music (Mrs. Wood played both the organ and the piano) and family singing. Ayer cousins frequently came for Sunday dinner. There were sleigh rides in winter, pony-cart jauntings and picnics in summer. If the weather was inclement, there was marshmallow toasting at one of the many fireplaces in the house, and Dad would tell one or two of his favorite tales. Sunday also meant Sunday school lessons with Mother.

As the four children reached school age, they were sent off to boarding schools. The boys attended elementary grades at the Noble and Greenough School in Boston's Back Bay. Afterwards, their parents sought to enroll them at the Groton School, but the headmaster, Reverend Endicott Peabody, replied that the school could not take additional boarders. The boys were then enrolled at St. George's School in Newport, Rhode Island.[7] The younger son later transferred from St. George's to Middlesex School in Concord, Massachusetts. Rosalind was enrolled at the Master's School in Dobbs Ferry, New York.[8] Irene, the youngest, attended Miss White's School for Girls in Paris, France.[9]

The children apparently were good students. William Jr. won the highest honors in Latin at St. George's, where he also was a member of the varsity football team. Cornelius excelled in mathematics. After prep school, the two boys went to Harvard College. The older son majored in sociology, and Cornelius, upon his father's advice, majored in English. William Wood had promised each of his sons $1,000 if they would not drink or smoke until they had reached the age of twenty-one. Cornelius made an earnest effort, but William Jr. joked, "What's the use? We'll get the $1,000 anyway!"[10] The older son was a handsome blond with blue-gray eyes, whose good humor was as infectious as his sunny disposition. He was his father's favorite.

The elder Wood had grand plans for both of his sons. After graduation from Harvard, they would join the American Woolen Company. Eventually, William Jr. would succeed to the presidency when the elder Wood retired. Cornelius would assume the position of executive vice-president. At least, those were the father's hopes.

While the boys were still at the Noble and Greenough School, Wood set about buying up the 600-acre island of Cuttyhunk. Situated off the southeast coast of Massachusetts, Cuttyhunk is the western-most island of the Elizabeth Islands and is located five or six miles from Martha's Vineyard. Exactly what propelled Wood to undertake such a venture is not known. The August 6, 1959, issue of the *America's Textile Reporter* offered the fascinating, albeit unsubstantiated, explanation that Wood's Portuguese heritage prompted the purchase. According to the article, Wood's father (identified as Manuel Silva) was a Cuttyhunk fisherman. It is known that in 1867, when William Wood was nine years old, his father took him for his first visit to the island. Perhaps when William Wood became a wealthy man, he purchased the island for sentimental reasons.[11]

Cornelius Wood later recalled of his father: "Dad was never able to do things on a small scale. . . . When Dad got the building urge there was no stopping him. The sky was the limit."[12] Cuttyhunk was typical. Here, in 1913, Wood designed and built a second summer home. On the highest point of the island he erected a large, rambling, frame residence with twelve bedrooms, a billiard room, two bowling alleys, and an immense living room. A large picture window in the living room commanded a spectacular view of Martha's Vineyard, William Wood's birthplace. Tons of clay fill were carted to the top of the hill for a tennis court. A 120-foot mast from a wrecked schooner was erected in front of the building as a flagpole. Some distance beyond the main house, Wood decided to build a great stone castle. When the children learned that this single architectural adventure would cost $600,000, they persuaded their father to settle for something less grandiose and considerably less expensive.[13] The three-story, fieldstone house that Wood built in place of the castle was nonetheless an enormous structure. He named it The Winter House. Rosalind and her father called the estate on Cuttyhunk, Avalon.[14] In summer the children sailed and swam here with their college friends.

In 1908, Frederick Ayer gave to his daughter Ellen Wheaton Ayer Wood a beautiful estate on Paine Avenue at Pride's Crossing near Beverly, Massachusetts. She named it Woodstock.[15] It was but a mile or so from her father's palatial, Italian Renaissance villa on Massachusetts' north shore. Woodstock became another home away from home for the family.

Mrs. Wood and the children spent part of most winters in Florida. Although she was of somewhat delicate health, she managed to supervise governesses, maids, luggage, and the children on these frequent pilgrimages to the nation's newest resort area.[16] Rarely was Wood able to go with his family to Florida.[17] He did, however, make the trip in January 1923, and while in Palm Beach, he commissioned Addison Mizner to build a mansion facing the ocean.

The circumstances surrounding the construction of still another mansion reveal the idiosyncrasies of Wood's interest in building. Mizner, at the time, was Florida's most popular architect for rich American families. When he inquired of Wood, "What type of overall design do you prefer," Wood replied, "I kind of like towers." He instructed Mizner to build, decorate, and furnish the residence throughout, complete with silverware, china, and wine cellar.

The Towers, Wood's Palm Beach Mansion, Florida (1924). Addison Mizner, architect. (Courtesy of the Historical Society of Palm Beach County)

He even left the hiring of the servants in the architect's hands. As Wood wrote out a check, he tersely remarked, "I will arrive for dinner at 8 o'clock on December 15, 1924 and when I get here I want a hot meal on the table!"[18] Mizner was flabbergasted. He nonetheless carried out the assignment within the stipulated period. True to his word, Wood arrived at the Towers promptly at 8:00 P.M. on December 15, and Mizner's large staff of servants served dinner. The cost of the structure, which boasted twenty servants' rooms alone, was in the neighborhood of $625,000.

In addition to the trips to Florida, the Wood family enjoyed other travels. They periodically visited Europe, where William Wood combined business with sight-seeing. He usually took along one of his limousines and his favorite chauffeur on these expeditions. One summer, Mr. and Mrs. Wood hired a sumptuous, private Pullman car with drawing rooms and took Rosalind and Irene on a grand tour of the United States. The girls invited school chums and favorite cousins to accompany them.[19]

As the children grew older, beaux began calling on Rosalind and Irene; and William Jr. and Cornelius started dating young debutantes in Boston and the North Shore area. Marriage became a topic of family conversation. No doubt the frequency of such discussions increased after the lavish wedding of Mrs. Wood's younger half-sister, Beatrice Banning Ayer, on May 26, 1910. Guests traveled from Boston to Frederick Ayer's estate at Pride's Crossing by private train. A reception and dance followed the ceremony at St. John's Church at Beverly Farms. The groom was a handsome young graduate of West Point named Second Lieutenant George S. Patton.[20] Inasmuch as the marriage took place on a Thursday afternoon, William Wood did not attend with the rest of his family. His workweek continued the customary six days.

Between 1915 and 1917, three of the Wood children were married. Cornelius at the age of twenty-one was the first. On December 15, 1915, he and Muriel Prindle were married in Duluth, Minnesota. William Jr. married Edith Gainsborough Robinson in Louisville, Kentucky, on February 10, 1916. In January 1917, Irene ("Tot" as her mother and father called their youngest child) married Captain Bernard Sutcliffe of Halifax, England, in New York City. Not to be outdone by his father-in-law, William Wood hired private Pullman cars to transport the friends and relatives from the Boston area. For each of the three young couples there were generous wedding gifts from the parents. Rosalind ("Diddah" as her family called her) did not marry until much later. In 1927 she married Count Francesco Mario Guardabassi.

In the competition between William Jr. and Cornelius for who would produce the first grandchild, the older brother and his wife won.[21] Doris Anne

William Madison Wood, Jr. (1918).
(*Booster*, September, 1922.
Courtesy of Lawrence Public Library)

Cornelius Ayer Wood (1919).
(*Booster,* October, 1922.
Courtesy of Lawrence Public Library)

Worthington Wood was born on October 20, 1916, at Arden. A second child
was named William Madison Wood III. Cornelius and Muriel had two children, Muriel and Cornelius Jr. Rosalind and her husband had two sons, Ginnio
and Frederick. Irene and Bernard did not have any children. The prospect
of grandchildren gave William Wood another excuse to build. At the time of
William Jr.'s marriage in early 1916, Wood had already started the construction of still another mansion. Located 150 yards south of Arden, it was completed by late 1916. Wood gave it to his namesake and his daughter-in-law
Edith.[22]

A description of this three-story, stucco edifice done in the Spanish
Colonial Revival style again illustrates Wood's lavishness in building. The
enormous building had a green tiled roof with dormers and exterior chimneys.
There was a porte-cochère entry vestibule with Palladian-inspired doorway.
Perley S. Gilbert was the architect. The interior of the building had matched,
quartered-oak paneling throughout all three floors (there were an additional
two levels underground). Banisters and moldings on the two staircases were

Orlando Cottage, built on Wood's estate, Arden, for
Mr. and Mrs. William M. Wood, Jr. (Author's collection)

hand carved. The lighting fixtures were silver. There were six bedrooms, each
with its own private bath. The servants' quarters were on the third floor. On
the main level were several drawing rooms, a living room, a game room,
butlers' pantries, and an enormous dining room. The seventy-by-thirty-five-
foot dining room boasted a carved mahogany table that could seat fifty dinner
guests, and a huge, hand-woven oriental rug that covered the entire floor. The
ceilings on the first floor were of hand-molded plaster with festoons of gar-
lands and rosettes. Wood had imported several Roman plaster craftsmen to
do the ceilings and two German cabinetmakers to do the hand-carved wood-
work. A large modern kitchen with a walk-in cold room was connected to the
dining room above by a large dumbwaiter. Formal gardens surrounded this
architectural showpiece. The Woods modestly named it Orlando Cottage.
"The amount of money that went into this house was unbelievable," Cornelius
Wood later wrote.[23] The sum of $400,000 may not be too far off the mark.

Cornelius and his bride moved into what was called the Lake Cottage on
the Arden estate. They considerably enlarged and modernized the residence,
and although it was not so large and ornate as Orlando Cottage, it was a
commodious, livable dwelling. Wood undoubtedly helped his younger son
with the renovation, by, as usual, sparing no expense. It was not that William
Wood was a reckless spendthrift; he simply believed that his children were
entitled to every convenience and luxury that his great wealth could provide.

Wood's belief that his family deserved the best of everything reflected
how very important they were to him. He was an intensely private man by

52

nature, and it was only with his wife and children that he was able to relax. His hobbies were ones that could be enjoyed while he was with his family. He was an omnivorous reader, with a particular interest in history, and he was fond of classical music and Italian operas. On one occasion the children remember him playing "O Solo Mio" fourteen times straight on the gramophone at Arden.[24] While he was not a sportsman, he did enjoy sailing. Both of his sons shared their father's love of the sea, and he indulged them both with yachts.[25] He gave his children many other expensive gifts as well, including Rolls Royces for William Jr. and Cornelius. When Rosalind decided to move to New York City in 1916, her father installed her in a luxurious apartment at the corner of 53rd Street and Park Avenue. His generosity was not limited to his wife (in her own right a wealthy woman) and his children. For his mother, he built a spacious home in Woburn, Massachusetts. For his two remaining sisters, he built large homes—one for Emma in Scituate and another for Susan in North Reading, Massachusetts—where they lived out their long lives in ease and comfort.[26] For his younger brother Otis, Wood regularly purchased annuities.

Wood's largesse also extended beyond his family. For example, after his death it was learned that he had advanced at least $600,000 to various individuals who never repaid the loans.[27] William Madison Wood, the cost-conscious master of the American Woolen Company, was apparently incapable of saying no to an acquaintance down on his luck. Many of the loans had been for hospital and burial expenses. Others had been made to young men who, like Wood several years earlier, hoped to succeed in their particular endeavors; unlike Wood, however, their dreams presumably never materialized.

At times, Wood's generosity overlapped with his compulsion to build. In 1908 he erected the imposing granite arch at the entrance of West Parish Cemetery in Andover in memory of one of his young proteges, Benjamin Franklin Smith, who had died at the age of twenty-one.[28] In the cemetery itself, Wood built a charming stone and brick chapel with a carved interior and Tiffany stained-glass windows. Along the edge of the cemetery, he erected a handsome wall of pink granite. When he learned that the roof of the West Parish Church needed repairs in 1910, he arranged for the installation of an attractive red tile roof.[29]

What sort of man was this intensely family-oriented individual who was, at the same time, the driving force behind the largest woolen corporation in the world? In religion, he and his family were members of the Episcopal church. When in Andover, they worshipped at Christ Church, where the three younger children were baptized. In politics, Wood was a rock-ribbed

Republican. In 1896, as a member of the Massachusetts delegation to the state Republican convention, he cast his vote for William McKinley as presidential candidate. Furthermore, he was a protectionist who favored high tariffs, especially on woolen fabrics. He was an advocate of unrestricted immigration because the busy mills of his vast organization were frequently in need of inexpensive, unskilled labor. He belonged to the New York Yacht Club, the Union League and Metropolitan Club of New York City, the Algonquin Club of Boston, and the Brookline Country Club. Additionally, he was vice-president of both the National Association of Wool Manufacturers and the Home Market Club. He also served as a director of various national banks, including the Chase National, the largest bank in the United States. These are facts readily found in *Who's Who,* but they do not really tell us much about the man himself.

That he dearly loved his family has been shown. That he was a wealthy man—indeed, a millionaire by the early twentieth century—goes without saying. His generosity was legendary in the Merrimack Valley. Yet he still remains something of a mystery figure. As an executive of the American Woolen Company, he made headlines in the nation's business and financial journals, and occasionally, a leading popular magazine would run a feature article on him. Personal details were rarely mentioned, however. It was not that he shunned publicity—anything that put the name of the American Woolen Company before the public pleased him—but interviewers were rarely permitted to probe beyond his remarkable business career.

Contemporaries of Wood, most of them admiring, some of them critical, give us perhaps the best portrait of the man. Physically, he was short and of dark complexion. He tended to be somewhat heavyset, and he wore pince-nez glasses as he grew older. His bushy eyebrows surmounted dark, piercing eyes. He was a meticulous dresser who fancied spats and carried a cane. He smoked fine Havana cigars. The traditional gold watch chain was customarily looped across his ample waist. He had the proverbial Latin temperament, which was awesome to witness. His younger son described such explosions: "Once in a while the work would get him down. Then he would 'blow his top'. When he did, it was like a violent squall with thunder and lightning. The earth trembled; at least we [children] did."[30] If such a temper could be vented in his own home, the office scenes must have been of earthquake dimensions. But he was quick to regret these tirades. A kind word or a pat on the back was his way of apologizing.

He could be brusque, almost to the point of rudeness. Those closest to him were the ones to bear the brunt of his occasional incivility. But there were so

54

many things that he had to decide each day that his aides generally understood and forgave his curtness. He drove himself at such a near-killing pace that he was prone to be impatient with more fallible individuals. He also was arbitrary in dealing with his associates. Yet his personal kindness and his generosity were another side of Wood's personality. One of his obituaries described him as "a peculiar compound of despot and philanthropist."[31]

In order to understand the man, it is essential to recognize that he had two loves in his life. His first love, above all else, was his family; his second love was the American Woolen Company. As he had dreamed of creating this giant corporation in the 1890s, so, in the early twentieth century, he dreamed of his son and namesake becoming his successor. His family and his corporation—he viewed both as his creations. As paterfamilias, he expected the firm to be passed on in the Wood family. This was not unusual for such corporate magnates; John D. Rockefeller and Henry Ford had identical dreams.

It is worth recalling here that William Madison Wood was born of poor, at times almost destitute, Portuguese parents. The first twenty-odd years of his life scarcely gave a clue as to what would happen in his later years—his association with Frederick Ayer, his marriage into one of New England's wealthiest families, and his earning a salary the envy of many a man his social superior. Then followed the founding of the American Woolen Company and his phenomenal rise to fame and fortune.

All this was surely heady stuff for a man who never forgot the days when he earned four dollars a week. As he moved into the highest financial and industrial circles of the land, he took on the accoutrements of this newly-found social world. Retinues of servants, palatial homes here and there, Ivy League college for his sons, yachts and limousines, private Pullman cars, and exclusive social and business clubs—they were all part and parcel of Thorstein Veblen's scathing indictment of "conspicuous consumption," which he penned in his 1899 classic, *The Theory of the Leisure Class*.[32]

This heretical and highly original work criticized business and middle-class values of the day. Written about the United States in perhaps the sleaziest decades of its history—an America of money-lust and greed, of men of power whose flamboyant pecuniary values were emulated by the whole American people—it exposed the hollowness of many of the nation's canons of taste, education, dress, and culture. Veblen attacked the conspicuous consumption of the "leisure class": its lavish expenditures that satisfied no real need but were only marks of prestige. Then, as today, this ethos prevailed especially among the *nouveau riche*. Veblen believed that this group used these trappings of aristocracy as a substitute for position by birth.

Who would need to prove his position more than Wood, the son of Portuguese immigrants? He seems to have taken on the accoutrements of his newly-found social world with a vengeance. Apparently it was important to him that he be accepted. As he piled luxury upon luxury, he could then rationalize that he rightly belonged to the highest circles of American society. His fascination for building mansions supports this generalization. Perhaps these luxurious homes were his way of compensating for the drab and cramped quarters in which he had been born and had grown up. Perhaps they also were a way for the son of immigrants to prove to the social class in which he now lived that he was one of them.

And yet, that Wood was included in this category is ironic, for the man who created and directed the American Woolen Company rarely knew much leisure in his entire business career. His only relaxation was, as a friend observed, "work and more work." His work was directed toward making the giant firm a successful undertaking. Aside from his family, the firm would dominate his time and interest for the next quarter-century of its corporate life.

CHAPTER IV

Empire Builder

ALTHOUGH Frederick Ayer had been named president of the newly-formed American Woolen Company in 1899, Wood, as treasurer, was the driving force behind the organization. As mentioned earlier, the eight firms that initially merged had shown average net profits of $2,593,000 for the two years preceding the combination. During the first five years (1899–1904), the consolidation averaged profits of only $2,900,000 a year, not too promising a beginning for such an ambitious undertaking.[1]

Competition was the name of the game in the woolen and worsted industry in those years, and it was upon competition that the American Woolen Company fed and grew strong. Wood and his organization methodically acquired additional mills. Month after month, year after year, the acquisitions continued.[2] By the time of Wood's retirement at the end of 1924, the American Woolen Company owned and operated some sixty mills with a work force of 40,000 employees. By that date, it was recognized not only as the nation's largest woolen manufacturing concern but also as the world's greatest textile corporation. Yet it was no trust or monopoly in the popular meaning of these terms. Not even in its heyday of high production and large profits did it ever produce more than 20 percent of the nation's woolen and worsted fabrics. It always faced the full competition of hundreds of rival firms which made the other 80 percent of the fabrics. That is not to say, however, that its power in

Contemporary photograph
of the American Woolen
Company headquarters,
245 State Street,
Boston, Massachusetts.
(Photograph by Clarisse
Poirier)

the field of men's-wear goods (particularly in blue serge) was not especially
great.

> The proportion of its equipment to the total of such machinery in the country
> was estimated to be "very large . . . more specifically at about 70 percent for . . .
> worsted goods, and about 50 percent for . . . woolens." With respect to these
> lines, the position of the Company must be admitted to have been one bordering
> on quasi-monopoly, and suggested the possibility of considerable influence by
> the Company in the control of the market for such fabrics.[3]

It was not bigness for its own sake that drove Wood to build this vast
manufacturing empire. As previously mentioned, he appreciated the advantages of such a consolidation. A large working capital—the largest in the
industry—would make possible the installation of the newest, most efficient
machinery and the creation of a research division to develop, invent, and keep
an eye open for any improvement of machinery or manufacturing process.
The resulting efficiency would enable the firm to produce an increasingly
better quality of goods in larger quantities. With more and better goods, the
company could undercut competitors and capture a lion's share of the market.

Following these steps to success was not always easy. Wood himself provided an illustration of the day-to-day problems he tackled in the early years

of the American Woolen Company.[4] At a staff meeting, he fixed the price of a certain fabric at so much a yard. He based the price on the proven efficiency of a particular mill's machinery and on the assumed efficiency of a specified number of weavers. The public liked the fabric and sales were brisk. But the efficiency of the weavers proved to be a problem; production per weaver was not as high as expected. The experience taught Wood that well-trained mill hands were essential to cost efficiency. Thereafter, it was common for the firm to hire 400 men and women as "green hands" and train them for several months in order to get a minimum of 40 good weavers. The necessity of keeping the plant's machinery operating at full capacity, however, usually resulted in assigning the rejected trainees to semi-skilled jobs elsewhere in the mill. Here it was the job of the supervisory personnel to watch them carefully and to prevent their lack of skill from interfering with the output of fabrics.

Directing and managing the unprecedented growth of a woolen textile firm from eight to sixty mills required tremendous skills and determination.

William Madison Wood in his office at 245 State Street, Boston, Massachusetts. Circa 1914. (*McClure's*, August, 1914)

William Wood was equal to the task. He was an indefatigable worker; a seventeen-hour workday was normal. More importantly, he was organized and he was decisive. In 1923 he told an interviewer that years before he had visited Henry Saltonstall of the Pacific Mills in Lawrence. He found him studying a mill report at a desk that was absolutely bare except for a blotter, a pen, and an ink well. Wood recalled:

> I went back to my office and started to clean up everything that was on my desk. There was such an accumulation of papers that I hardly knew where to begin. Before night I had disposed of the whole batch. Having cleaned my own house, I was in a position to demand that the men around me clean theirs. We have continued to observe that rule pretty faithfully.[5]

Wood's own office was a model of efficiency in spite of the constant jangling of telephones. Aside from the photographs of business associates on the walls, it was spartan in decor. Two secretaries took his rapid-fire dictation. A bank of phones kept him in touch with his staff of executives spread throughout New England and New York. In a single hour, Wood could issue enough orders and directives to keep his key assistants busy for a week. A limousine was always standing by to whisk him to any trouble spot in the vast organization. He admitted that without the telephone and the automobile his task would have been well-nigh impossible.

Many a night, lights in his second-floor bedroom at Arden burned until three or four in the morning. Mill executives were often overnight guests, and they could be awakened at any hour and summoned to Wood's room. He kept a coffee pot at his bedside and between sips of the strong, black brew he would outline a major policy decision to a groggy aide. It would be up to the assistant to see that the plan was implemented the next day.

Some of his business associates thought that Wood was an impulsive man because of his tendency to make decisions quickly. He himself insisted that "decisiveness is more or less a mental habit" and that every executive worth his salt had to make quick decisions. That did not mean that the decisions were made impulsively, however.[6] When he detected that a mill was lagging in production, he immediately set about finding out what the trouble was. Either the machinery or the organization was at fault, and, more often than not, it was a flaw in the organization. Wood could no more abide inefficiency in an employee than he could abide a defect in a piece of mill machinery. Rapid advances in textile machinery design enabled him to get the highest rate of production possible. But building a staff of efficient executives was his overriding concern. He offered fine salaries and attracted many an experienced textile official from Philadelphia and New Jersey to the American

Woolen Company payroll. In-house promotions went to men who were innovative and efficient.

Many of his contemporaries considered Wood an autocrat. Every major decision was his and his alone in the years that he headed the corporation. He was once asked, "Don't you believe in team work?" His reply reveals much about the man.

> Of course I do. No one can get along without loyalty and cooperation. But, not all men are alike. I am what I am. Not perhaps what I would choose to be, but what I *am*. And in business I am a man that works alone, because I cannot work any other way. Most businessmen drift together in groups. . . . They are like a chariot team; two, four, six horses abreast. But I can't travel that way—hitched up with others. Whether I want to or not, I must travel alone. It is like breaking a path or blazing a trail. *One* man does it. . . . He may make mistakes. All he can do is to use his judgement, have the courage of his convictions, and keep on going! That's all I have done. It was the only thing I *could* do.[7]

A man long associated with Wood once observed, "As president of the American Woolen Company, he carried personal control to heights seldom, if ever, equalled."[8]

This control enabled Wood to put his own expertise to work for the company. He had an almost unerring faculty for judging market conditions, the trend of the money market, and wool prices. He knew the costs of goods down to the penny, from raw wool up through every phase of its manufacture into cloth. With this knowledge, he could control expenses and spot waste at every level of production. He knew exactly the price for which he could afford to sell tops and noils and other products of the mills. His competitors either based their prices on those set by the American Woolen Company or, more commonly, set arbitrary prices.

Wood's mastery of every facet of the wool manufacturing business proved extremely beneficial for his firm. In 1908 he developed an apparatus for testing the percentages of moisture and other foreign matter in raw wool.[9] With this information, American Woolen buyers could quickly calculate the exact amount of shrinkage that would occur in any lot of wool and thus determine which lots provided the most wool for the money. Inasmuch as the cost of raw wool constituted about 60 percent of the average value of cloth, a savings on its purchase offered a considerable advantage to Wood's giant concern. Additionally, Wood's contacts with wool growers from Australia to Wyoming were the envy of the industry. When he thought the time favorable, he ordered his buyers to contract for millions of pounds of raw wool, which were then stored in the firm's network of six-, seven-, and ten-story warehouses.[10]

Wood was responsible for still another advantage enjoyed by the American Woolen Company during most of its life. This was the unique selling arrangement that Wood had devised back in the late 1890s to turn Ayer's Washington Mills into a profitable operation. Shortly after its incorporation in March 1899, the new firm had its own sales department in New York City. In 1900 the American Woolen Company of New York, a wholly-owned subsidiary, was created to take complete control of all sales.[11] A sixteen-story office building was erected at 225 Fourth Avenue and 18th Street to house the new agency. Unlike the vast majority of its competitors, the American Woolen Company did not deal with commission houses in disposing of its woolen and worsted output. Instead, the goods were sold directly to customers. By eliminating the middleman, the firm was able to substantially cut selling costs. Indeed, by 1901, Wood's firm occupied so preeminent a position in the woolen industry, that "more and more the trade has come to depend upon 'the big company' for the direction of the industry in the following season [and] for setting the pace." Never again would William Wood have difficulty in securing bank credit. The power of the commission houses, however, apparently continued to be a factor with smaller woolen manufacturers.

Perhaps one of the most important benefits for the American Woolen Company derived from Wood's premise that a manufacturing organization of such a large size could achieve the greatest possible economies of production only by the installation and full utilization of the most modern machinery and overall plant design. Accordingly, money was freely spent in pursuance of such a goal. For the first five years, the firm regularly plowed earnings back into the business. Some $6,000,000 was expended for new machinery and construction. Still another $3,000,000 was earmarked for repairs and depreciation. Annual dividends on the company's preferred stock in these same years averaged $1,400,000, save for the year 1900 when they exceeded $2,300,000.[12]

Under Wood's careful eye, the American Woolen Company doubled its capacity in its first five years "by building a huge addition to the Assabet Mills, Maynard, Massachusetts, by acquiring several other mills, enlarging buildings, and improving their equipment. Increased business taxed even the capacity of the expanded mills and pointed to the need for more looms if earnings were to be further increased."[13]

In 1905, Wood decided to construct a huge, new plant across the Merrimack River from the Washington Mills in Lawrence. Destined to be the largest worsted mill in the world, this gargantuan structure was built in record time. "Cloth was being manufactured in April 1906, where a long line of willow trees and birches were swaying in the breezes of the previous April."[14]

Office building of the American Woolen Company of New York, sales headquarters of the parent firm. 225 Fourth Avenue and 18th Street, New York City. Built in 1910, this building served as American Woolen Company headquarters from 1931 to 1955. (Courtesy of Merrimack Valley Textile Museum)

Dubbed "the eighth wonder of the world" by residents of Lawrence because of its size, the building handled the entire job of manufacture, from raw wool to finished fabric. The new mill was designed to produce sufficient yarn for its own looms, and to provide many of the American Woolen Company constituent mill units with yarn that previously had to be purchased on the open market. As with the change in selling methods, this innovation was intended to give the corporation the fullest benefits of large-scale operations. Wood was not displeased when his board of directors voted to name this newest and most costly ($3,500,000) addition to the American Woolen Company facilities the Wood Worsted Mill in honor of the firm's newly elected president. Wood replaced his father-in-law as president after Ayer retired on June 8, 1905.

The new Wood Worsted Mill was a vast six-story structure containing thirty acres of floor space. There were sixteen miles of aisles lined with 230,000 spindles and 1,470 looms. A total of 7,000 mill hands were needed to operate this single plant. From every side came predictions of failure. Such a behemoth was too big to be manageable. It would be impossible, even for the American Woolen Company, to staff such a plant with competent supervisors. Wood had anticipated this problem, however. To prepare for proper staffing, he had instituted in the Washington Mills an elaborate system of understudies. For every official in the Washington Mills, from agent to superintendent, from overseer to foreman, there was, in training, an assistant. When the Wood Mill was ready to go into operation, the president issued a terse directive: "The entire organization of assistant executives will step over to the Wood Mill and assume the management there."[15] For its day, it was a coup in organizational management. Time would prove that William Wood had the qualification that Andrew Carnegie said was essential to success—a keenness in selecting the proper persons to manage and direct the business at hand.

A good indication of the difficulties of "the business at hand"—woolen manufacturing—was once described by Wood. He and Charles Schwab, the first president of the United States Steel Corporation, both served on the board of directors of Chase National Bank. They often compared business experiences. According to an account published by the American Woolen Company in *The Greatest Name in Woolens,* (there is no date or place of publication indicated), Wood once remarked to Schwab:

> Your steel business is simple. You dig your raw material of iron ore . . . in the Mesabi Range . . . pure, soft iron ore . . . haul it to Pittsburgh, and with a few operations you make it into pig iron . . . [and steel] . . . and sell it with no worries about chemical reactions or variables in the raw material and no styling problems. We in the American Woolen Company get our raw material from every country in the world, grown under different weather conditions, hundreds of thousands of different breeds of sheep, millions of different fleeces, all affected by the weather and by the health of the individual wool-bearing animals, all of different grades, different staples. We bring it to the mills and blend it according to seasonal changes and seasonal requirements, and we put it into hundreds of different yarns and thousands of different fabrics, and then of thousands of different patterns. The raw material and the manufacturing conditions are never standardized from day to day, or from year to year—it's the most intricate manufacturing business in the world.

Schwab quite possibly pointed out to Wood that steel making also had problems.

While the Wood Mill was under construction, the board of directors voted in July 1905 to issue the $5,000,000 of preferred stock remaining in the treasury.[16] With this action, capitalization was increased to $54,501,000. Two years later in 1907, capitalization was further increased by an additional $10,000,000. Whether this considerable increase in capitalization was justified is doubtful. The original 1899 capitalization, which consisted of $20,000,000 preferred and $29,500,000 of common stock, represented assets in the plant account of some $40,000,000. These financial maneuvers of Wood's were apparently designed to over-capitalize the company. The preferred stock

64

covered the whole value of the firm's assets. The common stock was largely, if not entirely, pure "water." However, in the years that followed, the American Woolen Company built up its assets far beyond its capitalization and continued to gather under its wing many other companies within the industry. Indeed, an authoritative source has written, ". . . the situation compares favorably with that of other combinations of the period; and the existence of this surplus valuation may well have acted as a spur to more conservative financial management in the later years."[17] Over-capitalization was a common practice in this period of American capitalism. For example, in 1901 when J. P. Morgan created the United States Steel Corporation with an initial capitalization of $1.4 billion, fully one-third of this sum was over-capitalization.

Although Wood's American Woolen Company included some of the most valuable woolen fabricating properties in the nation, his combination had the initial burden of having to earn far more per loom than the rest of the industry before it could pay attractive dividends to its investors. An examination of the firm's balance sheets for its early years reveals a considerable and relatively steady increase of surplus, amounting to 50 percent on the outstanding common stock by 1911. Wood apparently devoted the firm's funds to the reduction of this capitalization, writing off $9,500,000 in that year. Additionally, he spent very large sums of capital on the acquisition of new machinery. His policy with regard to financing the erection of new mills was somewhat unorthodox. For such purposes a new corporation was, in each case, created. The officials of these corporations were American Woolen Company executives. Funds for the actual building of at least two mills were secured by the sale of the parent company's notes or bonds. The accounts of the new mills and their profits were kept separate until these obligations were paid off. With this sort of complex financial management, it was obviously necessary for each of the firm's looms to produce a larger output than the rest of the industry before it could pay attractive dividends. In the formative years between 1899 and 1906, William Wood, Charles Fletcher, and James Phillips, Jr., the firm's three-man executive committee, kept annual dividends below $1,750,000 (save in the year 1900 when they exceeded $2,300,000). The increased revenues were carried on the books as surplus. Wood thus was able to carry through his expensive plans for increased productivity and plant expansion and improvement. Holders of American Woolen preferred stock apparently accepted their annual 7 percent return in anticipation of better days to come.

The American Woolen Company began 1907 at a high rate of production, but the pace slowed as several breaks in Wall Street in March and again in August were followed by a financial panic. There was a series of runs on

The Wood Mill, Lawrence, Massachusetts.
(Courtesy of Merrimack Valley Textile Museum)

banks, and the number of commercial bankruptcies mounted. Many observers feared it would be a replay of the financial disasters of 1893, which had heralded a severe depression. As the hysteria spread, many merchants flatly refused delivery of the American Woolen fabrics they had earlier ordered. Finished goods piled up throughout the mills, and Wood ordered a sharp reduction in operations. Longer credit had to be granted to some customers caught in financial straits. Losses, many of them sizable, had to be shouldered when collections could not be made.[18] Net profits for the company dropped some 30 percent from the previous year. Yet in 1907 the company paid dividends that were up some 40 percent over those of 1906. This rise reflected the 1907 increase in capitalization. Wood apparently thought 1907 was little more than a dark cloud which would rapidly dissolve as trade conditions stabilized.

Some help in dissipating the cloud came when the second administration of Theodore Roosevelt changed the service uniform of the United States Army from the blue of the Civil War days to olive drab. Wood ordered his chemists to tackle the challenge. Within months, the Washington Mills in Lawrence turned out a run of the new fabric, which the government promptly approved and adopted. At the time, government orders were not particularly

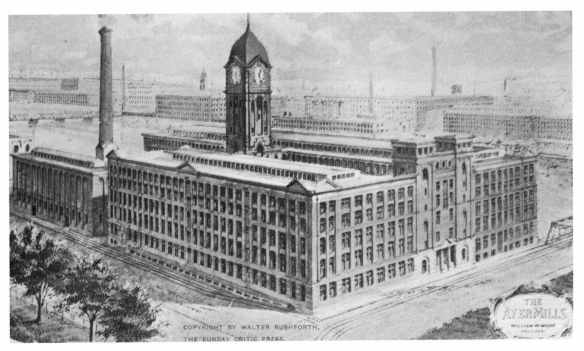

The Ayer Mill, Lawrence, Massachusetts.
(Courtesy of Merrimack Valley Textile Museum)

important to Wood. Within ten years, however, these orders would net the American Woolen Company a fortune.

In anticipation of improved business conditions, the president of American Woolen decided that he would put an end to a practice that his cost-efficient mind abhorred. A few constituent mills still had to buy their yarn on the open market; surplus yarn from the great Wood Worsted Mill was simply insufficient. In 1909 construction of the Ayer Mill (named in honor of his father-in-law) was started across the street from the Wood Mill. Once completed, this new yarn mill, the largest of its kind in the world, would end the company's need to secure yarn on the open market.

The year 1909, when William Howard Taft assumed the presidency of the United States, was the American Woolen Company's best and most profitable year since its inception. By now the company owned thirty groups of mills with 775 sets of cards and 8,000 looms. The Tenth Annual Report was a glowing account of past achievements with hints of still brighter years ahead. Aggregate business during the first decade amounted to $424,536,030, of which $37,107,559 represented net profits. The preferred-stock holders had earned $18,800,000. The sum of $10,514,808 had been accumulated and was carried as surplus. For depreciation, $7,986,374 had been written off. Wages had been increased 25 percent in the years between 1899 and 1909. The good news for the future was that the great Ayer Mill would be in operation by the following year.

A huge clock tower on the Ayer Mill dominated the skyline of Lawrence, which by 1910 was the acknowledged worsted center of the world, and the American Woolen Company dominated the industrial life of the city itself. Directing and dominating the huge corporation was William Madison Wood. As the great Ayer clock ticked away the hours of early 1912, a veritable explosion of labor unrest and violence rocked the city.[19] Overnight, Lawrence made the front pages of the nation's newspapers. Within weeks, "Wood was the most execrated man in America. . . . From the Atlantic to the Pacific, I was held up to the public as an object of hatred," he later confessed.[20]

The spontaneous walkout that started the great Lawrence strike of 1912 took place on the afternoon of Thursday, January 11. It is necessary to examine the background of this action to understand Wood's role in it. During this time in American history, a ground swell of support for political, social, and economic reform swept across the nation, mainly among the middle class. Historians have termed this phenomenon the Progressive Movement. In part, it was a reaction to the growing power of big business and the grinding poverty of so much of the nation's working class.

In late 1911 the state legislature of Massachusetts, caught up in this humanitarian agitation, voted to limit the workweek for women and children to fifty-four hours. The state's textile mills normally operated on a fifty-six-hour week. The law went into effect on January 1, 1912. In Lawrence, Wood and the other mill owners reduced the hours and wages accordingly. Inasmuch as the mills could not operate without a full complement of workers, the reduction was extended to include all employees: men, women, and children. For the majority of the operatives in the city, this resulted in an average loss of $.30 from their weekly pay envelope. According to an investigation made by the United States commissioner of labor, $8.76—about $.15 or $.16 an hour—was the average weekly wage of mill operatives at the time of the strike.[21] As paymasters distributed the envelopes, a cry of protest went up from workers in the Everett Mill. In a babble of foreign languages, the lament was the same, "Not enough pay!" Across the city's great mill district, thousands more joined in the protest. In some mills, angry workers slashed belts, smashed machinery, broke windows, and poured into the streets.

For the next six weeks, Lawrence witnessed one of the most egregious labor conflicts in American industrial history. Mayor John Scanlon's police

68

force was unable to cope with the "riot-ridden" situation. As a result, Governor Eugene Foss, who himself owned textile mills, ordered state militia into the city to help control the 30,000 strikers. The unorganized strikers responded by inviting the International Workers of the World (I. W. W.), a radical labor organization, to come to Lawrence to take charge of the movement.

The mill owners were adamant in their refusal to deal with the various strike groups. A meeting might be construed as tacit recognition of labor's right to organize, which the owners unalterably opposed. The only union in Lawrence at the time of the strike was an affiliate of the American Federation of Labor, the United Textile Workers Union, whose membership was limited to a few hundred skilled workers. William Wood and William Whitman, president of the Arlington Mills—two of the most powerful industrialists in the city—insisted that they paid "as much as they could—more than other industries—and that the immutable law of supply and demand decided such matters anyway."[22]

As the conflict dragged on, yellow journalists and muck rakers poured into

1912 Strike Poster, Lawrence, Massachusetts.
(Courtesy of Tamiment Institute, New York University)

A PROCLAMATION!
IS MASSACHUSETTS IN AMERICA?

Military Law Declared in Massachusetts!
Habeas Corpus Denied in Massachusetts!
Free Speech Throttled in Massachusetts!
Free Assemblage Outlawed in Massachusetts!
Unlawful Seizure of Persons in Massachusetts!
Unwarranted Search of Homes in Massachusetts!
Right to Bear Arms Questioned in Massachusetts!
Mill Owners Resort to Dynamite Plots and Violence in Massachusetts!

Ready to plunge the bayonets into woman's blood.

Militia Hired to Break Strike in Massachusetts!
Innocent People Killed by Militia in Massachusetts!
Militia Ordered to Shoot to Kill in Mass.!

Unusual Bail and Fines Exacted in Massachusetts!
Corporations Control Administrations in Mass.!

The striking textile workers of Lawrence, Massachusetts are confronted with the above described conditions. They are making a noble fight for an increase of wages and to prevent discriminations against the members of the organization carrying on this strike. To abolish a pernicious premium system inaugurated for no other purpose than the speeding up of already overworked toilers. If you want to assist the strikers send funds to JOSEPH BEDARD, 9 Mason Street, Franco-Belgian Hall, Financial Secretary Textile Workers Industrial Union, Lawrence, Massachusetts.

the city of Lawrence. Their sensational, often lurid, accounts of the strike situation were devoured by readers across the land. Headlines such as "Soldiers Bayonet Hungry Strikers" were matched by conservative articles captioned "A Reign of Terror in an American City" and "Smash the Machinery." To those who supported the workers, William Wood epitomized the robber barons of the wool trust. Many business and church leaders, on the other hand, decried the brutal violence of the strikers and branded the I. W. W. "our country's greatest danger."

"Lawrence, Massachusetts was America in microcosm," wrote one historian.[23] The city's population was 86,000; 86 percent were immigrants or children of immigrants.[24] Some forty-five languages were spoken by this polyglot mass of humanity. Between 1905 and 1910, as the Wood and Ayer Mills were being built, 15,000 immigrants flooded into Lawrence in search of employment. Most of the newcomers were Italians, Lithuanians, Poles, and Syrians, but there were also smaller groups of Portuguese, Armenians, and Franco-Belgians. As these new immigrants brushed against the older immigrant groups of Scots, Germans, English, Irish, and French Canadians, racial, ethnic, and religious tensions mounted.

Within a fifteen-minute walk of the great mill buildings that lined the

Tenement alley in Lawrence, Massachusetts, 1911. (Courtesy of Merrimack Valley Textile Museum)

Model housing built by Wood for American Woolen Company employees, Lawrence, Massachusetts. (Courtesy of Merrimack Valley Textile Museum)

North and South Canals of Lawrence was a sprawling collection of wooden, three-decker, noissome tenements. "Vile beyond description," these hovels housed as many as 300 to 600 people per acre.[25] A survey done in 1911 shockingly revealed the squalid living conditions of most of the city's population. Observers who visited the congested area reported "vermin, filthy alleys, voracious rats and evil smells."[26] At the time of the strike, the mean age at death in Lawrence was a bare fifteen.[27] And by fifteen, many a boy and girl had already been a mill hand for one or two years.

So appalling were these descriptions of living conditions in "the woolen capital of the world" that First Lady Mrs. William Howard Taft and other prominent Progressives visited the strife-torn city to see the situation at first hand. Perhaps the Reverend Adolf Berle of Tufts College voiced the view of most reform-minded Americans when he declaimed, "Somebody is doing a satanic wrong."[28] For many of the strikers and those who sympathized with their plight, that "somebody" was William Madison Wood.

He was stunned and angered by the criticism that was heaped upon him. He pointed to the thirty-six wooden tenements and forty-two brick flats that he had built for American Woolen Company employees in Lawrence, as evidence of his concern for the welfare of his workers. While it is true that

71

they were a residential showcase of the city, they housed less than one-tenth of 1 percent of his workers. Additionally, occupancy of these low-renting, company houses was, by-and-large, restricted to office and supervisory personnel of the Wood Worsted Mill. Indeed, the censure directed against him was not unjustified. Like the other industrial leaders of Lawrence (as well as of the country as a whole) Wood "had lost touch with the people on the payroll."[29] During the twelve years prior to the 1912 strike, he had been so obsessed with consolidating and expanding the operations of the American Woolen Company, that he had, as it were, lived in a world of profit and loss figures. The real world in which his 25,000 mill operatives toiled and sickened was beyond his knowledge or imagination. The vile smells and filth of the tenement district had never reached his Arden estate in Andover. It is doubtful that Wood had ever driven, let alone walked, along the pitiful streets and alleys that were home to most of his employees. Coupled with this total lack of awareness was his conviction that a handful of outside radical agitators had organized the strike. At the outset of the strike he had remarked that "justice [was] not on their side."[30] He was determined to break the strike and discredit the I. W. W. leaders.

Wood, in these early years of the twentieth century, was intensely anti-union, as were most American industrial leaders. Many of them shared the view expressed in 1902 by George F. Baer, president of the Philadelphia and Reading Railway Company, that unions were not needed: "The rights and interests of the laboring man will be protected and cared for—not by the labor agitators, but by the Christian men to whom God in his infinite wisdom has given the control of the property interests of the country, and upon the successful Management of which so much depends."[31] Indeed, Donald Cole, in his history of Lawrence, writes that the great Wood Mill was built in Lawrence in 1905 for the very reason that there was an "absence of unionism" in the area.[32]

Serious trouble began for Wood when an attempt was made by certain individuals to discredit the strike leaders and their followers. Lawrence police, acting on a tip, uncovered a cache of dynamite in the Syrian tenement district in late January 1912. The strikers disclaimed responsibility and argued that "mill interests" had planted it. Police later arrested Andover contractor Ernest Pittman, who had built the Wood Mill, and Lawrence funeral director and school committeeman John J. Breen for planting the explosives. In a poorly documented series of events, Pittman supposedly confessed (while drunk) to authorities that he had provided the dynamite for Breen and Wood. On August 27, 1912, Pittman took his own life. The case against Breen was so

William Madison Wood, about 1912.
(Courtesy of Merrimack Valley Textile Museum)

clear that the attorney general's office bound him over to the grand jury; he was later convicted and fined $500. Attorney General Joseph C. Pelletier then had William Wood and two others indicted for conspiracy to plant dynamite. Not even Pittman's confession and a corroboration from Breen were enough to convince the Suffolk Superior Criminal Court jury that Wood was involved in the plot. On the morning of June 7, 1913, after deliberating throughout the night, the Boston jury acquitted Wood of the charge of conspiracy to injure the textile strikers at Lawrence by planting dynamite. Later that same day, Wood gave out the following statement:

> I am profoundly grateful for the verdict which the jury has rendered in my behalf in the so-called dynamite case. I had no reason at any time to assume that

the verdict would be otherwise. I was not conscious of any guilt in connection with the alleged conspiracy because I was in no way implicated in it nor did I have any knowledge of it.

I was given a fair trial. . . . The grand jury having found an indictment against me and the others, Mr. Pelletier felt it his duty to press the case for trial and the best possible vindication that could come to me was through the verdict by the jury. It has been a long and hard ordeal to pass through. . . .[33]

As the strike continued through February 1912, Wood abandoned his own "stand firm" advice to his fellow mill owners. He met with a delegation from the strike committee on March 1 and offered a 5 percent wage increase. The group wanted additional benefits. On March 9, Wood met with them again and offered raises up to 11 percent. Again they held out for more. Three days later, Wood and the other mill owners capitulated. Raises ranging from 20 percent for the most poorly paid operatives to 5 percent for better paid hands were offered. An additional 25 percent was promised for all overtime. No striker would lose his or her job for having taken part in the prolonged conflict. The committee agreed and the cheers that greeted their announcement of the settlement echoed from a mass rally on the Lawrence Commons. Within days, the mills resumed operation.

All in all, the strike had been a harrowing experience for everyone concerned, including William Wood. As a contemporary and acquaintance of Wood wrote, "It was truly an ordeal through which to pass; but from it he learned some things which served him well in later years."[34] His social conscience, which had slumbered these many years, had been rudely awakened.

Of great assistance in making Wood conscious of his duty to his employees, as well as to the stockholders of the American Woolen Company, was his elder son, William Jr. At the time of the strike, the twenty-year-old youth was an undergraduate at Harvard College. He followed the Boston press accounts of the conflict and talked with his father on weekend visits to Arden. He majored in sociology at Harvard and had taken a number of courses in economics and industrial relations. William Jr.'s professors had apparently instructed him in the necessity and desirability of cooperation between management and labor if the nation was to avoid the class conflict and industrial warfare that the I. W. W. urged. The president of the American Woolen Company had "always maintained that the interests of capital and labor coincided, and not even radicals doubted his sincerity."[35] It took William Jr.'s advice to convince the elder Wood that the initiative for better labor relations had to emanate from management's side.

After graduating from Harvard in 1915, William Jr. joined the American

MORE THAN A PLACE TO WORK

This center-fold from the American Woolen Company's employees' magazine
illustrates Wood's enlightened industrial relations program, inaugurated
in 1919. The children in the bottom center photograph are swimming
in Hussey's Pond, Shawsheen Village, Andover, Massachusetts.
(Courtesy of Lawrence Public Library)

Woolen Company. His plans for a farsighted company welfare program and
other schemes to benefit employees—or perhaps allay labor unrest—were
interrupted by America's entry into World War I in April 1917. Following the
conclusion of the conflict, William Wood gave his namesake carte blanche to
establish an industrial relations department.[36] An employees' news magazine
The [American Woolen] Employee's Booster started publication in 1919. In
the same year, a day-care nursery was built in Lawrence for children whose
mothers worked in the firm's mills, and a summer camp for employees' children was opened in Boxford, Massachusetts. Social and athletic organizations
were financed and equipped with American Woolen Company funds. The
Homestead Association, a wholly-owned subsidiary, was established in 1919

Children of mill operatives in an American Woolen Company truck,
Lawrence, Massachusetts. (*Booster*, September 1920. Courtesy of
Lawrence Public Library)

to permit employees to buy (on the installment plan) company-built houses
at cost. In 1920 still other imaginative benefits—together with wage increases—were introduced. "In its treatment of labor, the American Woolen
Company may fairly be said to be a leader in the industry . . . far-sighted as
compared with most of its competitors . . . ahead of the great majority. . . ."[37]
Slowly, the bitter memories of the 1912 strike faded against the new background of better wages and enlightened labor/management relations.[38] Perhaps these admittedly praiseworthy measures were also a way to counter any
possible move by employees to organize an effective union. Not until the 1930s
and 1940s did the Textile Clothing Workers Union wage successful organizational drives among employees of the American Woolen Company.

In the years that followed the 1912 upheaval, contemporaries noted that
Wood actually craved the confidence and cooperation of his "fellow workers,"
as he now termed the mill operatives.[39] He did win, to an amazing degree,
their trust and cooperation. Indeed, in the years following the conclusion of
World War I, the firm reported, "his popularity among the workers of the
company was phenomenal."[40] When, in 1919, the United States Bureau of
Labor Statistics revealed that the cost of living in Lawrence was higher than
in forty-three other cities of similar size east of the Mississippi River, Wood
ordered an investigation. He learned that certain storekeepers in Lawrence
raised their prices whenever wages at the mills were increased. Wood issued
an "ultimatum" to the merchants of the city. If that practice did not stop at

once, he would open American Woolen Company department and grocery store facilities in the city. The merchants backed down. When Wood next visited Lawrence in 1920, "the crowd of twenty thousand mill workers, which greeted him, held up his automobile . . . they greeted Mr. Wood as their economic savior."[41] No doubt many in the throng had viewed Wood in quite a different light in 1912. While it must be admitted that the company's public relations and labor relations departments played up these "manifestations" for all they were worth, there nonetheless may have been a genuine spontaneity in these public demonstrations on Wood's behalf.

Wood may have basked in this newly found popularity, but pressing tasks and challenges increasingly occupied his time and attention. In 1913 a prolonged strike of garment workers in New York City necessitated reduced operations by the firm's mills. President Woodrow Wilson in the same year convened a special session of Congress to revise the tariff on woolen and cotton cloth downward. This economic threat unsettled the industry for the greater part of the year. Wilson's public attack on the "insidious" tariff lobby on May 26, did little to endear the Democratic leader to Wood and his fellow protectionists. On October 3, 1913, the Underwood-Simmons Tariff Act became law. While still protectionist in principle, schedules were 10 percent lower than in the Payne-Aldrich Tariff of 1909. Additionally, duties were lowered on fabrics. The 1912 surplus of $12,000,000 on American Woolen Company books dropped to $8,000,000 by the end of 1913, as company profits dipped and dividend payments ate into cash reserves.

The year 1914 "was one of peculiar difficulty in the wool business."[42] Foreign imports flooded the domestic market at a rate four times greater than in the previous year. In addition, there was a general depression in business and growing unemployment. Wood attempted to build an export business in worsted and woolen goods, but was unsuccessful. Low foreign production costs, together with cheap labor abroad hampered sales. He told his board of directors, "Our efforts must . . . be directed to securing to ourselves the market of the United States, the best and greatest market in existence."[43] At the time, the company's capital amounted to $60,000,000, which was 14 percent of a total of $415,000,000 invested in wool manufacture in the United States.

In spite of the difficulties of 1914, the company was able to earn within $11,398 of the entire dividend of $2,800,000 paid upon the preferred stock. It is significant that under Wood's presidency the American Woolen Company never failed to pay an annual dividend on its preferred stock. Wood's salary in 1914 was $100,000. The income from his personal investments and large real estate holdings is not known.

In August 1914, Wood was the subject of a lengthy article in *McClure Magazine*'s feature series "Stories of Hundred Thousand Dollar Salaries." Edward Mott Woolley's essay was entitled "Driving Forty Mills For $100,000 A Year." It was an apt title. Wood, who was now fifty-six years old, drove himself at a pace that few of his younger assistants could equal. On infrequent occasions, however, he did take a vacation. In August 1914, he was on a combined business and sight-seeing trip to Europe when the Great War, as it was then termed, broke out. Wood found himself right in the midst of opening hostilities. Apparently he was in Belgium as the German army launched its attack. His limousine was confiscated by German authorities, and he hurried back to the United States.[44]

For the next four years, the armies of the Allies (Great Britain, France, Russia, and Italy) struggled with the powerful forces of the Central Powers (Germany, Austro-Hungary, and the Ottoman Empire). On land, the conflict turned into a bloody stalemate. On the high seas, German submarines sank hundreds of thousands of tons of Allied and neutral shipping. President Wilson issued a proclamation of United States neutrality on August 5, 1914. Americans followed the war news in the nation's press but went about their daily business.

Initially, the outbreak of hostilities had an unsettling effect on an already nervous American business community. Gradually, however, economic activity picked up in 1915 as Great Britain and France and, to a lesser degree, Russia and Italy placed orders for foodstuffs, explosives, and other war materials. American Woolen shared in this unexpected bounty. There were substantial orders for woolen uniforms and blankets from the Allied governments.[45] Additionally, the firm enjoyed considerable increases in domestic orders in 1915. By the end of the year, the company had unfilled orders amounting to $40,550,000 on its books.[46]

The spectre of a wool famine haunted Wood and other woolen and worsted manufacturers with the outbreak of the European war. Foreign wool, particularly from Australia, New Zealand, and South Africa, became difficult to obtain because of the scarcity of British merchant shipping and the growing depredations of German U-boats. The manufacturers urged American farmers to raise more sheep, but domestic wool supplies proved inadequate, both in quantity and in quality of fibers.[47] Wood, with his usual foresight, assumed that the wool situation would worsen in the years ahead. In 1915 he urged his board of directors to purchase as much wool as possible at the prevailing prices. In a rare instance of noncompliance, the board strongly opposed his suggestion and refused to sanction the purchase. Angered by this

78

rebuff, Wood told them that he personally would purchase and store huge quantities of wool.[48] The following year, wool prices increased from 30 to 65 percent over those prevailing at the close of 1915. Wood then sold his large wool holdings to American Woolen. It is not known at what price he disposed of the wool—the price he had paid for it in 1915, or the considerably higher 1916 prices.

The mills of the great corporation hummed with activity throughout 1916. Orders, both domestic and foreign, were up 40 percent over the previous year. Net profits of $8,210,761 were the largest in the firm's seventeen-year history. On April 15, 1916, the common stock of the company, which had never previously paid dividends, was placed on a 5 percent dividend basis.[49] The annual preferred dividend continued at its regular 7 percent. On February 15, 1916, all properties of the American Woolen Company, originally incorporated under the laws of New Jersey, were transferred to a new corporation organized under the laws of Massachusetts. Wood had made this decision so that the stockholders (most of whom were residents of the Bay State) would no longer have to pay taxes on their dividends, as they did under New Jersey tax laws.

The giant firm, now with a total of fifty mills and 10,000 looms, had the capacity to absorb the unprecedented volume of orders that poured in during 1916. Enormous unfilled orders were on the books. Most of them were domestic orders resulting from the increased purchasing power of Americans. There was also a substantial number of foreign civilian orders from regions formerly supplied by the mills of Europe. Production had virtually ceased at many European mills because of the fierce fighting in their localities. Wood declared at the end of 1916 that his company's prospects had never been brighter.

The entry of the United States into the war against Germany on April 6, 1917, inaugurated tremendous business activity throughout the nation. Wood saw to it that the American Woolen Company shared in the bonanza of war-time profits. He dispatched William Jr. to Washington to secure government contracts for uniforms and blankets. Competition was keen; Amoskeag, of New Hampshire, J. P. Stevens, of New York, the Pacific and Arlington Mills of Lawrence, as well as foreign firms, all placed their bids with government purchasing boards. Despite the rivalry, William Jr. "landed the largest [$50,000,000] single textile order that had ever been allocated [by the United States government]."[50] Such a monolithic order could produce huge profits for the American Woolen Company, even though their price bid was lower than that of any other competitor. By the end of 1917 the firm had received an additional $52,000,000 in United States government orders.

Meanwhile, the government had commandeered the entire stock of raw wool that was in dealers' hands or that had been contracted for abroad. The emergency measure forced mill owners to rely mainly on their warehoused supplies of raw wool for manufacturing civilian goods. The American Woolen Company storehouses still contained sufficient supplies of wool for its non-military purposes. As for the large quantities of wool needed to fill the government orders, Washington allocated more than enough to the firm. One half of all the machinery in the fifty mills was engaged in filling Army and Navy orders. In spite of the deluge of government contracts, production of fabrics for the civilian market occupied almost half of the firm's employees. Net profits for 1917 totalled $15,664,985 — almost double those of 1916. Part of the profit increase was due to an expansion of markets. Prior to America's entry into the war, the American Woolen Products Company had been incorporated to carry on a general export business.[51] On April 1, 1917, branch offices were opened in Canada, Cuba, Mexico, five South American nations, and the Far East. Despite a scarcity of shipping, this subsidiary exported cloth valued in excess of $1,300,000 in 1917.

The wartime prosperity continued into 1918. Net profits were $12,324,084. Dividends on company stock were up 25 percent over those of 1917. Almost $20,000,000 was carried as surplus on the company's books. Wood and his giant concern were riding high. On March 14, 1918, Frederick Ayer died at the age of ninety-six. Although Wood undoubtedly mourned the death of his father-in-law, he also must have welcomed the chance to bring one of his dreams closer to realization. William Madison Wood, Jr. succeeded his grandfather as vice-president and became a member of the board of directors of the American Woolen Company. In addition to these new responsibilities, William Jr. joined the United States Naval Reserves. His brother Cornelius became a United States naval officer on active duty.

The American Woolen Company's wartime profits of 1917 and 1918 were equalled in 1919, even though the war had ended. Net profits for the latter year were $15,513,414. Some $30,000,000 were now on the books as surplus. Dividends on both preferred and common stock were up 25 percent over the previous year. The 18,000 stockholders were delighted. Wages for the firm's 40,000 employees were increased approximately 30 percent and the workweek was reduced from fifty-four to forty-eight hours. Group life insurance and sickness, accident, and maternity benefits were inaugurated with the American Woolen Company bearing the entire costs of these measures. The Homestead Association accelerated its building program of low-financed houses for employees. William Jr.'s enlightened policy of labor/management relations was the talk of the textile world.[52] William Wood, Sr. also shared in these prosperous times. As president of the corporation, his salary and commissions for 1919 totalled $548,132. In addition, the company paid "any and all income taxes, State and Federal" for Wood and all the officers of the company.[53]

Despite fluctuations in the price of raw wool and despite cancellations of some buyers' orders (in anticipation of lower prices), American Woolen Company mills operated at near full capacity. This was at a time when "two-fifths of the broad looms in the country were idle."[54] The American Woolen Products Company increased its export sales by 100 percent during 1919. Unfilled orders amounted to $4,800,000. The parent company declined to accept an additional $12,000,000 in foreign orders because the mills were unable to fill them.[55] The same mills that had turned out millions of khaki uniforms for the United States Armed Forces during the war years now poured out miïes of blue serge suiting for the returning doughboys. Blue serge was the staple product of the American Woolen Company, just as the black Model-T was the principal product of the Ford Motor Company in 1919.

The success of Wood's woolen empire was due almost entirely to the man himself—to his driving ambition, his boldness, his imagination, and his remarkable organizational skills. Behind these personal characteristics was Wood's insatiable thirst for more mills, more customers, more power, and more profits. Despite the hectic business activity of the American Woolen Company in the years from 1917 through 1919, William Wood occasionally found time to think of another dream that intrigued him. He planned to build a model corporate community for the company's managerial and office force. Frye Village in Andover, Massachusetts, was to be the site of this novel experiment.

CHAPTER V

Shawsheen Village: Dream Turned Reality

Exactly why William Wood dreamed of creating a residential community for the managerial staff of the American Woolen Company may never be fully known. Certainly his intense interest in building and architecture must have played a part in this desire. Perhaps another reason stemmed from his view of himself as paterfamilias to both his family and company. An entire village —built and maintained according to his every whim and desire—clearly reflects such paternalistic ambition and pride. Whatever his motivation, the idyllic village that blossomed under his supervision stands as a landmark in early twentieth century American suburban planning and development.

As to how or from where he got the idea of the project, there are no answers, only conjectures. It is possible that as he walked about the wide veranda of the main house at Arden and looked down upon the farmland and swamps of Frye Village, the concept emerged full-blown from his fertile imagination. More likely, however, this well-read and well-traveled, inquisitive man developed the idea from a popular urban planning movement that had swept across western Europe and washed up on the intellectual shores of the United States during the Progressive Era. The nation's popular magazines carried accounts of these experiments in town planning in England, Germany, and elsewhere.

What helped to trigger this sudden interest in town planning in the

United States was a simple demographic fact. In 1920 the long-term movement of the country's population from rural to urban areas crested. The city and the factory now dominated the lives of most Americans. The full impact of the urbanization and industrialization of the nation was vividly apparent in the city of Lawrence. As previously mentioned, this carefully planned textile town had evolved into an industrial city of almost 40,000 people before the turn of the century. By the closing years of World War I, its population had more than doubled. Most of the 40,000 mill operatives (the majority of whom were immigrants or the children of immigrants) lived in unsanitary, crowded, wooden tenements. Like Topsy, Lawrence had "just grow'd and grow'd." Across the land, similiar scenes of industrial and urban blight marched hand in hand with technological advances and increased corporate profits and dividends.

This same scenario had earlier unfolded in Great Britain during the reign of Queen Victoria (1837–1901) as England led the western world into the industrial age. A small coterie of British social reformers and town planners, led by such farsighted individuals as Sir Ebenezer Howard (1850–1928) and Sir Raymond Unwin (1863–1940), conceived and implemented the concept of "garden cities" as a solution to the relentless sprawl of urban-industrial ugliness. These individuals believed that modern industrial technology did not require the aggregation of countless people in large cities and towns. Air, light, greenery and dispersal from congested industrial locales were essential ingredients in their planning.

Ebenezer Howard in 1919 defined a "garden city" as a "town designed for healthy living and industry; of a size that makes possible a full measure of social life, but not larger; surrounded by a rural belt. . . ."[1] His plans called for a garden city having a maximum population of 30,000 people on 1,000 acres. There were to be residential, commercial, industrial, and recreational zones. The population was to be a balanced mixture of all social groups and levels of income. The whole of the town acreage was to be in public ownership or held in trust for the community. Surrounding the model town was to be a country belt of 5,000 acres with 2,000 agrarian inhabitants.

The actual pioneers in the development of these model "garden cities" were English manufacturers. In 1879 the Cadbury family started construction of Bournville (completed in 1895) for workers in their chocolate factories. Port Sunlight was begun in 1888 by the Lever family, manufacturers of soap. Both communities, with their variety of residences, parks, tree-lined streets, and advanced ideas of factory designs and locations, played major roles in the evolution of the "garden city" concept. In the early twentieth century the theory was incorporated into the two most famous examples of early British town planning: Letchworth, started in 1904, and Welwyn, started in 1920. Both of these "garden cities" were within an hour's journey of London (as was Wood's community so positioned in relation to Boston). Thanks to the electric streetcar and the internal combustion engine, the ideal marriage of town and country was now considered possible.

The "garden city" concept soon became the basis for a new movement in urban reform in the United States, although the original idea underwent several adaptations as it gained in popularity. Many American planners tended to push for the more limited "garden suburb" as better suited to immediate, widespread application. This was a much more modest scheme than that of Howard and Unwin. The land would be privately owned and the emphasis was to be upon private residential units rather than multifamily tenements. The "garden suburbs" would be developed by private enterprise and would feature efficient land-use, low population density, and provision for recreational needs. These residential "garden suburbs" would be located in the countryside within commuting distance of the place of work of the inhabitants. The proponents argued that this union of rural and urban life would resolve one of the most troublesome paradoxes of American civilization—namely, the worship of countrified life in a land dominated by urban civilization.

There are several possible sources for Wood's knowledge of the new movement. In the years between the establishment of Letchworth and the building of Welwyn, Wood was an occasional visitor to the British Isles and Europe. Fascinated as he was with architecture and building and perhaps influenced by the sociological and labor/management relations theories that his elder son had acquired at Harvard, the president of the American Woolen Company must surely have heard about and been intrigued by the "garden city" and "garden suburb" concept.

Wood had already built some 200 houses in Lawrence and elsewhere, many of which were sold on easy terms to "blue collar" employees of the American Woolen Company. James E. Allen, a leading Lawrence architect, had designed many of these workers' homes, and quite possibly he was aware of the exciting experiments in town planning then underway in Great Britain. Perhaps he discussed the concept with Wood. Whatever the cause, Wood's interest in company housing was well known.[2]

Still another possible source for William Wood's knowledge of the movement was an adaptation of the concept devised by the federal government. During the course of World War I, a housing shortage had developed in the

United States; it was especially severe along the eastern seaboard. The shortage of housing in industrial centers, "even before the United States entered the war in 1917, made it imperative for the government to plan and construct housing estates for munitions workers and shipbuilding workers. . . ".[3] The Black Rock development at Bridgeport, Connecticut, and Yorkship Village near Camden, New Jersey, both government housing developments, caught the attention of social-minded architects and industrialists throughout the country because of the planning concepts utilized in the units. While these developments were not considered "garden cities," they did offer certain amenities such as recreational areas, curved streets, and orderly housing. In 1919, the very year that Wood began to build Shawsheen Village, the government published the *Report of the United States Housing Corporation* (Vol. II, Houses, Site Planning, Utilities. Washington: Government Printing Office, 1919). This landmark in the literature of American architecture and town planning was of interest not only to architects and town planners, but also to manufacturers and agencies devoted to social betterment, philanthropy, and civic improvement. It was a fascinating picture book of plans and perspectives for new communities. It seems doubtful that this particular publication would have escaped Wood's sharp eye, especially since he was well aware of both the housing shortage in the metropolitan Boston area and the high rentals being charged employees of the American Woolen Company.

Taking all these factors into consideration, it is difficult to believe that this perceptive, dynamic textile magnate was unaware of the movement by town planners, social reformers, and government agencies to create a new urban-industrial environment for the twentieth century. "An environment," in the words of Lewis Mumford, that "dared put beauty as one of the imperative needs of a planned environment: the beauty of ordered buildings, measured to the human scale, of trees and flowering plants, and of open greens surrounded by buildings of low density, so that children may scamper over them, to add to both their use and loveliness. . . ".[4]

Shawsheen Village, which Wood built between 1919 and 1924, was not a "garden city" in the pure sense of the term. It more resembled a "satellite suburb." The very nature of its geographical location identifies Shawsheen Village as a hybrid. Built on the site of Frye Village, which was a part of the town of Andover, Wood's model creation was located less than three miles from the center of the city of Lawrence. Indeed, the northern limits of Shawsheen Village in the 1920s were within walking distance of South Lawrence. To the west and east of the village, there was green space aplenty (along Lowell and Haverhill Streets), but to the south and north, Andover and

Lawrence were almost cheek by jowl with Wood's corporate community. The ctiy of Boston itself was but twenty-five miles distant. Yet, in spite of its closeness to these urban industrial areas, Shawsheen Village with its green lawns, parks, playing fields, tree-lined streets and golf course seemed a "fairy-land" to local residents and visitors alike.

Frye Village, at the time Wood first established a residence there, was a part of the New England town of Andover. The seventeenth-century origins of Andover in the Massachusetts Bay Colony followed the customary procedure of the land-hungry English settlers who had pushed westward from the coastal settlements of Salem and Ipswich. The Indian tribes that roamed the vicinity of the Merrimack and Shawsheen rivers had only the vaguest concep-tion of the English theory of real estate holding. These New England red men no more grasped the full impact of signing an agreement with the white man than did their Manhattan brethren who sold their island to Peter Minuit for twenty-four dollars worth of trinkets. The local Indians received six pounds and a cloth coat for their land.[5] Shortly after the consummation of this real estate bargain, Andover was duly incorporated as a township on May 6, 1646.

In 1718 a man named Samuel Frye, a descendent of John Frye, one of the original freeholders of Andover, built a saw and grist mill along the west bank of the Shawsheen River a mile or so north of Andover's South Parish. Such was the unpretentious origin of Frye Village. From its first day, the small community was influenced by industry.

By the time Andover celebrated its two-hundredth anniversary, Frye Village boasted a thriving flax industry, the first of its kind in America. John Smith and his younger brother Peter, fleeing the grinding poverty of Brechin, Scotland, settled in Frye Village in the early nineteenth century. In 1824 they built a mill along the Shawsheen for the manufacture of machinery used in cotton mills. Nine years later they were joined by an old friend from Brechin, John Dove. It was Dove who convinced the Smith brothers that they should experiment with the processing of flax. In 1836 they constructed a mill along the west bank of the river. The operation was successful, and the firm of Smith & Dove soon became noted for its high quality fine thread, shoe thread, and sundry flaxen products.

Still other industries developed in Frye Village. Elijah Hussey built another saw mill on a large mill pond. In 1833, William and Jonathan Poor opened a wagon manufacturing plant across the street from Joseph Poor's blacksmith shop. William Donald started an ink shop elsewhere in the village.

Smith and Dove Flax Mills, Frye Village, Andover, Massachusetts. Note the wide mill pond in foreground and the wooden bridge across the Shawsheen River. (Courtesy of Society for the Preservation of New England Antiquities)

Frye Village, Andover, Massachusetts. The little girl is standing at the corner of Poor and Lowell Streets. The boys to the right stand beside Smith and Dove tenements. Village Hall is right rear. Village flag pole at left of photograph. Circa 1900. (Courtesy of Andover Historical Society)

By the 1830s the hamlet had developed its own character as a section of Andover and boasted its own village hall.

In the decades following the Civil War, Frye Village settled into an unhurried, crossroad community. The main thoroughfare, the Boston turnpike, was a dirt road scarred with wagon wheel ruts and horses' hoofprints. Intersecting it, in the village square, was the stagecoach highway from Haverhill to Lowell. An 1888 map of the village shows that some sixty structures, most of them wooden residential units, were located along the banks of the swift-flowing Shawsheen River. Here was the Andover Town Farm built by Jacob Chickering in 1837; it was an imposing brick-on-masonry structure done in the Greek Revival fashion.

By far the most imposing structure in all of Frye Village was the John Smith residence on the east side of the Boston Turnpike opposite the old Hussey homestead. Less than half a mile south of the Smith home, John Dove had Jacob Chickering design and build a large, rambling residence on the west side of the highway. It was this property that William Wood purchased and named Arden.

Frye Village, looking north on Haverhill Street. Village Hall to the right ("Smith and Dove Mfg. Co." sign above door). White residence to the left, property of J. W. Smith. Note square smokestack of Smith and Dove Mills in the background. (Courtesy of Society for the Preservation of New England Antiquities)

By the opening decade of the twentieth century, Frye Village had grown but slightly. The tiny cluster of buildings was surrounded by wide expanses of meadow, pasture, and swampland. The Shawsheen River meandered under overhanging alders and white birches on its way to join the Merrimack River at Lawrence. Village children attended classes in the three-room, red-brick schoolhouse and fished and swam in the Shawsheen River. Hunters bagged duck and small game. "Nothing ever happens in Frye Village. It was a place where it was always afternoon."[6] William Madison Wood would soon change all that.

Wood's plans for Frye Village were carefully spelled out. Here, in the country-side, he would build an entire community for his "white collar" employees: executives, agents, overseers, managers, wool buyers, and other salaried office personnel. They would both live and work there, for Wood intended to make the village the headquarters of the American Woolen Company. Wood also intended that his community serve as a model for other industrialists and social planners whose objectives were the same as his. In this planned environment, as a contemporary journalist wrote:

> it is hoped, that the office force, removed from the city with its distractions, artificiality and extravagance, will become attached to the country and learn its simplicity, its out-door life, freedom, wholesomeness and neighborliness . . . [here also] they can imbibe enthusiasm for the organization and live content-edly in comfortable dwellings among neighbors and friends.[7]

Wood's announced intention was "to lose no opportunity to promote wisely and justly the happiness and prosperity of those upon whom this great indus-try depends."[8] By relocating his managerial personnel to this idyllic locale, the president assumed they would be happy and content and thus would contribute even more to the success of the firm.

Wood's sociological concept of Shawsheen Village was elitist. In 1924 he directed the publication of a promotional brochure entitled "Shawsheen: The Model Community and the Home of the Offices and Staff of the American Woolen Co." One of the benefits listed in the brochure for executive and middle-management personnel illustrated a marked snobbishness: "Here their children have the advantages of education and association with boys and girls of their own type and breeding, where under ordinary conditions the child of the average office worker is denied such advantages."[9]

As envisioned by Wood, Shawsheen Village was to be both self-supporting and self-contained. This was not to be a philanthropic undertaking; Wood was, after all, an intensely practical businessman. There would be residential and recreational areas, a commercial district, and an industrial complex. Retail stores, personal services, transportation, an inn, and athletic facilities, were but some of the many amenities that would make the community self-contained. Best of all, in its creator's mind, Shawsheen Village would be a walking community; residents would be able to walk anywhere within the area in ten or twelve minutes. The cost of these plans would run into the millions of dollars, but the windfall profits of World War I had swollen the coffers of the American Woolen Company. Wood was determined to see his dream realized.

Starting in 1906, Wood slowly and methodically began to acquire property in the area.[10] Here and there, now and then, he encountered difficulties. Several Frye Village property owners flatly refused to sell. Still others, hearing that the American Woolen Company was involved, asked exorbitant prices. But Wood was a stubborn man and by 1918 he had acquired tracts of land totaling some fifteen hundred acres.[11] Of this considerable acreage, approximately one hundred fifty acres were located within Frye Village proper. Most of the remaining property was located west of the hamlet along the Lowell Turnpike.[12]

Wood was anything but a patient individual and he was eager to start building by 1918. Wartime restrictions, shortages of labor and material, and the company's preoccupation with government contracts abruptly ended on Armistice Day, November 11, 1918. Shortly thereafter, the sedate town of Andover (its population less than 8,000) echoed the sounds of steam shovels, concrete mixers, horse-drawn drays, and lumbering motor lorries. Under the direction of John Franklin, chief civil engineer, and a group of able architects, and through the labors of a small army of surveyors, carpenters, brick-layers, masons, plumbers, electricians, and excavation crews, Frye Village disappeared and Shawsheen Village was born. Frye Village was too modest a name for such a grandiose undertaking. With the approval of Andover town officials and United States postal authorities, Wood named his community Shawsheen Village after the Indian name for the river, which means Great Spring.[13]

While the new construction continued unabated into the early 1920s, a score or so of older buildings, which Wood had purchased earlier, were relocated and modernized. Many of them were attractive, well-built colonial structures. The almshouse of the Andover poor farm, a three-story, red-brick building, was remodeled into dormitory facilities for American Woolen Company clerical help. Several of the old mill buildings along the Shawsheen River were torn down. The nineteenth century dam was removed from the

Bird's-eye view (from top of smokestack) of Balmoral Playing Fields, tennis courts, Spa, Boy's Club and Bowling Green, Shawsheen Village, Andover, Massachusetts. The six houses in the lower left of the photograph were relocated to clear the site for the Executive Administration Building. (Author's collection)

river. The wide mill pond was thus eliminated and the river's course slightly changed by confining it within cement and stone walls.[14] Open brooks responsible for some of the swampland area were diverted into the river through sunken culverts. Some of the area east of the Shawsheen lay at the flood level of the river, and into this section were carted hundreds of tons of top soil to raise it above flood stage.[15] The completion of sewerage systems, the paving of streets, the laying out of sidewalks, the construction of two stone and cement bridges across the Shawsheen (one on Haverhill Street and the other on Balmoral Street), all took place within a remarkably short period of time. Yet there was nothing haphazard. Nothing was left to chance. Everything was carefully planned.

Wood directed the design and building of Shawsheen Village in the same fashion that he ran the American Woolen Company. It was a one-man show and he was both director and producer. Despite his duties as president of a giant textile conglomerate, he frequently checked on the progress of construction. Assisting him in the supervision of the undertaking was his private secretary, George M. Wallace, a young Scottish immigrant. Wallace was probably responsible for the Scottish and English names given to the streets: York, Balmoral, Argyle, Arundel, Burnham, Windsor, Kensington, Sterling, Dunbarton, Carlisle.[16]

The following anecdote clearly illustrates the autocratic nature of Wood's involvement with the rise of Shawsheen Village. In the summer of 1921 he had sailed aboard the SS *Aquitania* to study business conditions in Europe. Upon his return, he discovered that an entire street had been laid out and a number of houses erected in the wrong place. "Move those houses and eliminate the street," he told Wallace as he pointed his cane toward the offending site. Within a week, the buildings were relocated on their proper lots and the street was gone.[17]

In the remarkably short time of five years, Shawsheen Village was completed. As 1923 drew to a close, the *Andover Townsman* editorialized, "overnight the raw edges have disappeared . . . now one sees Shawsheen Village with a full appreciation of its impressiveness and beauty."[18] What the editor saw was a remarkable achievement in community design and execution. Here in Shawsheen Village had emerged "a scientifically and artistically planned village, the like of which exists nowhere else in this country, and perhaps with the exception of Port Sunlight, in England, in no other country on the globe. It instantly arrests the attention of all whose thoughts and activities are identified with civic projects."[19] Everything about Shawsheen Village bore the mark of the ambitious, innovative Wood. The residential, commercial, recreational, and industrial areas were exactly as he had envisioned.

Mr. and Mrs. George M. Wallace, vacationing in Scotland. Circa 1924. Wallace was Wood's private secretary and assisted in the supervision of the building of Shawsheen Village, Andover, Massachusetts. (Courtesy of James Wallace)

Residential Areas

There were two clearly delineated residential areas. Indeed, they quickly acquired local nicknames. "Brick Shawsheen" referred to the red-brick houses west of Main Street. These were the spacious homes of top management personnel. "White Shawsheen" designated the frame houses, most of which were located east of the river. Here were the more modest dwellings for middle management employees. All of the 251 residential units in the village were designed in the Colonial Revival style, which had become so popular during the course of World War I.[20] While the majority of the homes were wooden, others were brick or a combination of brick, stone, and wood. Some houses were imposing structures with sweeping lawns; others were built on a smaller scale and located on smaller, landscaped lots. Most were single residences, but here and there double houses added variety. The majority of the new residential units were designed by Adden & Parker, Clifford Allbright, Ripley & Le Boutillier, all Boston architectural firms, and James E. Allen, a leading architect of Lawrence.

Wood's liking for neatness and orderliness was everywhere apparent in residential Shawsheen. All telephone and electrical wiring was underground. There was a sunken garbage container at the rear entrance of each house. He forbade the construction of garages on private residential lots as "unsightly," even though the homes were for managerial personnel, many of whom owned

"White Shawsheen," Shawsheen Village, Andover, Massachusetts. Corner of York and Balmoral Streets. Village Hall (built in 1837) lower right corner of photograph. (Author's collection)

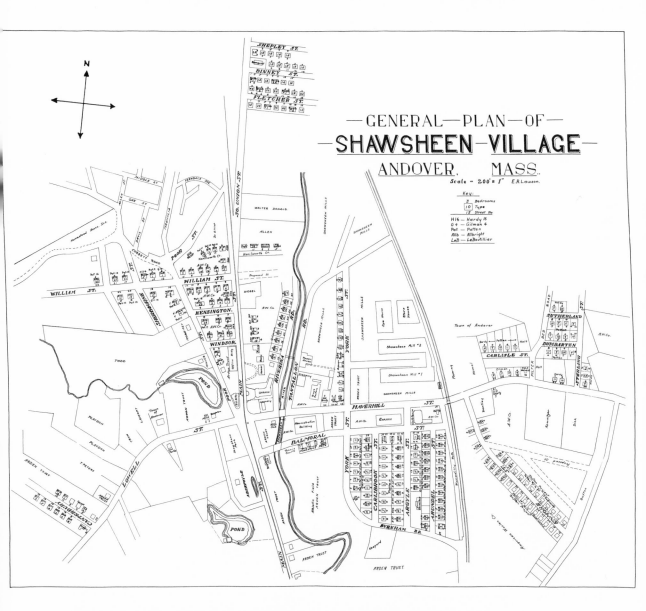

This detailed plan of Shawsheen Village was drawn by Edward R. Lawson, a clerk-draftsman in the Homestead Association. Undated, the plan was probably drawn between November, 1922 (when the Town of Andover voted to change the name of Warwick Street to William Street—in memory of William M. Wood, Jr.) and March, 1923 (when the Town of Andover voted to construct the Shawsheen Village grammar school in the area of Corbett, Poor, Magnolia, Middle and Allen Streets). Lawson's failure to include Adden & Parker and James E. Allen in the listing of architects and builders is puzzling. Close examination of the plan reveals that both architectural firms are keyed as designers of a number of residential units. Lawson's omission of the Shawsheen School itself may have been an oversight. (Courtesy of Andover Historical Society)

automobiles. Wood had forestalled any problems, however, by arranging for the construction of a large community garage in the village square.[21]

Wood personally selected the design of the streetlight fixtures and consulted with landscape architects as to the type and number of shrubs and trees to be planted. Stately old elm and maple trees were carefully dug up and replanted elsewhere if their original location interfered with his overall design. Even the two predominant colors for the residential structures, red and white, were by Wood's direction. "White Shawsheen" was exactly that. All of the houses were white with green shutters and blinds (miniature Ardens?). Despite the uniform whiteness of homes in this area of the village, the wide variety of different shapes and sizes made for a remarkably pleasing blend of individuality and harmony.

James E. Allen's architectural plans for the residential structures that he designed have been preserved. The specifications called for the use of the finest hardware, plumbing, heating, and electrical fixtures. This was in accordance with Wood's instructions that building contracts were not to be awarded to the lowest bidder but to firms noted for their high quality work. Allen's drawings specified sea-green slate roofing with copper flashing for the houses he designed in "Brick Shawsheen." Throughout the village, only the highest grade red bricks were used for construction. These "Kane-Gonic" bricks were made by the Goodrich Company, Epping, New Hampshire. This same brickyard had supplied much of the brick used in the building of the fashionable Boston Back Bay townhouses in the late nineteenth century. Allen's plans also contain designs for charming, individualized window shutters, exterior chimneys, handsome fireplace mantels, lead glass fanlights and striking main entrances. Housewives must surely have been delighted with

Architect James E. Allen's scale drawing of a residential dwelling, Shawsheen Village, Andover, Massachusetts. (Courtesy of Merrimack Valley Textile Museum)

his well-designed kitchen layouts and spacious linen closets with hinged drop-doors.

Screened side porches rather than front porches were the rule on all the houses in Shawsheen Village. And there was another rule: no fences were to be built in the residential districts. Many of the houses had window boxes. Employees of the Homestead Association regularly supplied residents with fresh, blooming plants.

The Homestead Association, an auxiliary of the American Woolen Company, handled all of the residential real estate transactions in the village. At a time when there was a widespread housing shortage in Massachusetts as well as in much of the nation, the rents charged in Shawsheen were only half the rentals being collected for similar housing in neighboring towns such as Reading, Stoneham, and Wilmington. The new occupants signed long-term leases with options to buy. In "White Shawsheen" rentals ranged from $40.50 to $48.50 monthly. Rentals for the more imposing red-brick structures averaged $125.50 monthly.[22] Those employees who opted to buy, and a few of them did so, paid anywhere from $4,000 to $15,000.

Commercial District

The self-containing aspect of Wood's overall concept of Shawsheen Village was most apparent in the commercial district, which was located primarily along Main Street in the vicinity of the square. Here were located the Post Office and Merchants' buildings, the Balmoral Spa, the Shawsheen Manor, and the community garage. Housed in these structures were such facilities as a first-class general store, retail shops, a bank, overnight and dining accommodations, a drug store, offices for business firms, and offices for doctors, dentists, lawyers, and architects. Additionally, there was a dairy and a laundry, together with barber, hairdressing, and tailor shops.

The unifying architectural theme of all the major commercial structures was either Tudor or Georgian Revival. These motifs made for a harmonious blend with the Colonial Revival design of the two residential areas. Adden & Parker designed the Post Office building, a two-and-one-half story, brick and limestone triangular structure on the corner of Poor and Main streets. Crowning this Georgian-Colonial edifice is a handsome clock-and-bell tower. In addition to the post office, the building housed the offices of the Homestead Association, a general store, legal offices of the American Woolen Company, and a large hall for social and civic meetings.[23] The latter was also the home of the Village kindergarten.

Post Office building, corner of Poor and North Main Streets,
Shawsheen Village, Andover, Massachusetts. (Author's collection)

Interior of Balmoral Spa, Shawsheen Village, Andover, Massachusetts.
(Courtesy of Andover Historical Society)

Shawsheen Manor, Shawsheen Village, Andover, Massachusetts.
Formerly the John Smith Mansion, Frye Village.
(*Booster*, April, 1921. Courtesy of Lawrence Public Library)

Across North Main Street from the Post Office, Adden & Parker designed a yellow-brick building decorated with three Doric columns and topped by a roof balustrade. This was the Shawsheen Garage, one of two such structures built to house and service the private automobiles of village residents. These garages also provided maintenance for American Woolen motor vehicles assigned to the village industrial complex.

The Balmoral Spa, located along the west bank of the Shawsheen River at the corner of North Main and Balmoral streets, was one of the most architecturally significant buildings in the village. Adden & Parker designed this two-and-one-half-story, red-brick, "U" shaped building in the Georgian Revival style. The ground floor housed the village drug store, an opulent establishment with marble columns and inlaid tile floors. On the second floor were located a barber shop, a hairdresser, additional offices, and a large public hall. The latter was used for dancing, occasional live theatre, and motion pictures.

In summer the Spa was the busiest building in the square. Its sidewalk terrace, with tables and gaily colored beach umbrellas, was located at the front of the building, facing Balmoral Street. At the other end was an outdoor dance pavilion with live music on weekends. At fifty-five cents per person, the pavilion quickly proved to be the most popular dance facility in the region. Along the bank of the river were docking facilities, canoes, and rowboats. A few yards to the south was the favorite swimming hole in the river. There was also a nine-hole putting green nearby. Wood was tremendously proud of the Spa and its facilities, which included outdoor tennis courts along the east bank of the river on Balmoral Street. He once boasted that the Spa was "the only place north of Boston where a man could buy a dollar cigar."[24]

Several hundred feet north of the Post Office building stood the Merchants' Building. Clifford Allbright, a Boston architect, designed this three-story, brick and granite structure. It provided space for numerous retail stores on the first floor and ample office accommodations on the upper floors for woolen firms doing business with the American Woolen Company. By 1926 the Andover Town Directory listed thirty-six wool business firms with offices in the building.

Opposite the Merchants' Building on North Main Street stood the Shawsheen Manor, which had been the residence of John Smith, founder of the old Smith and Dove firm. This was a first-class hostelry with large dining facilities as well as overnight accommodations. This three-story building had a mansard roof surmounted by a cupola and contained fifteen guest rooms, each with a fireplace. In 1922, twenty-five additional rooms were added. The Manor's dining room seated 200 persons; it also had lounges, a dance hall, and separate dining facilities for "chauffeurs of transients" and the staff.[25] The hostelry quickly earned a good reputation for its fine food and service.

Although the Post Office, Balmoral Spa, the Merchants' Building, Shawsheen Manor, and the Shawsheen Garage were located on North Main Street, the commercial area of the village also extended eastward on Haverhill Street to Tantallon Road. Here were located two handsome, two-story brick buildings. The Shawsheen Creamery provided dairy products for the residents as well as for the Spa and the Manor.[26] The Shawsheen Laundry supplied the finest linen and laundry service in the area. Inasmuch as Wood did not care to see wash fluttering in the backyards of his newly built residential units, village housewives were regular customers of the laundry.[27]

By far the most imposing structure on the square was the Executive Administration Building of the American Woolen Company. It stood on the east side of the Shawsheen River. Fronting the building was a sweeping flagstone terrace, which reached out toward the stream. Adden & Parker designed this striking four-story structure in the Georgian Revival fashion. Built of Indiana limestone and brick, it has eleven bays on the east and west facades and seventeen bays on the north and south. As might be expected, Wood wanted it to be the architectural capstone of the center of the village. More than 129,000 square feet in size, it housed the entire administrative headquarters of the American Woolen Company. Its interior was opulent: marble wainscot, oak-paneled walls, and cork floors in public corridors. There was a grand staircase inside the main entrance with inlaid marble flooring. On the lower level of the building was an auditorium that seated 300 persons. The executive suites were almost baronial. They had baroque designs carved on the ceilings and over the doorways, the fireplaces were built with marble facings, and the chandeliers were made of hand-wrought pewter. Wood's presidential suite occupied rooms 310–312. Above the first-floor windows at the front of the building was an ornamental frieze, which repeated, in stone, the ram's head (symbol of the American Woolen Company), the American eagle, and the Shawsheen Indian.

Across the river, in front of the Executive Administration Building, was located a small stone structure. According to local legend, William Wood, while on a 1918 visit to Valley Forge, Pennsylvania, had toured the 1777 winter headquarters of George Washington's Continental Army and had been impressed with a certain stone building. Upon Wood's return to Andover, he directed that an exact replica be built to serve as a boys' club and polling booth. Adden & Parker were the architects. It was built of fieldstone with a

The Executive Administration Building of the American
Woolen Company, Shawsheen Village, Andover, Massachusetts.
(Courtesy of Merrimack Valley Textile Museum)

tiled gable roof and massive end-wall chimneys. Whether Wood thought he
was building a replica of Washington's headquarters (which it definitely is
not) or whether he built it out of genuine patriotism is a moot point.[28] Although it is the smallest structure in Shawsheen Village, it is as architecturally
attractive as the twentieth-century community which surrounds it.

Recreational Facilities

Even though Wood was not a sportsman, he took pains to provide exceptional athletic and recreational facilities for the residents of Shawsheen Village. The Balmoral Playing Fields stretched for acres along the eastern bank
of the river. Here were located soccer, football, and baseball fields, a quarter-
mile track, and a grandstand seating 5,000 persons. As mentioned earlier,
there were tennis courts and a putting green on Balmoral Street. In winter
the courts and the infield of the track area were flooded for hockey and ice
skating. At the corner of North Main and Haverhill streets, directly to the
west of the Boys' Club, Wood had laid out a manicured bowling green, which
became a popular gathering spot for older residents who preferred something
less strenuous than a tennis match or a soccer game. Swimming facilities were
provided at Hussey's Pond, directly across Poor Street from the Post Office.
In 1921, Wood had the pond drained and a concrete bottom laid. Bathing
houses were built, and summer swimming and winter skating soon became

a regular part of village life. A mile west of Shawsheen Village, a championship, eighteen-hole golf course was laid out by W. H. Follet, a Boston landscape architect.[29] Additionally, there were facilities for dancing, live theatre, and movies.

Industrial Complex

Central to Wood's planned corporate community for managerial personnel was the great Shawsheen Mill complex itself. It was located on Haverhill Street west of the Boston & Maine Railroad line. Here was a five-story, brick and concrete power plant with a tall, round smokestack. The plant provided steam heat and electrical power for all the commercial and industrial buildings in the village. The Shawsheen Brush Mill, just east of the creamery on Haverhill Street, manufactured textile brushes and also contained a large wood mill and woodworking shop that provided the paneling and lumber for all of the commercial buildings and many of the residences. These mills were still other indications of Wood's determination that the village be self-contained. Also located on Haverhill Street was the second American Woolen Company garage, a three-story, brick and cement structure designed by the firm's engineering department. This building provided auto storage facilities for the residents of "White Shawsheen."

Dominating the entire village were the Shawsheen Woolen Mills Nos. 1 and 2 together with a ten-story, octagonal wool warehouse and dyehouse. The warehouse could hold forty-million pounds of wool. This complex was

Shawsheen Mills Nos. 1 and 2, Shawsheen Village, Andover, Massachusetts.
(Courtesy of Merrimack Valley Textile Museum)

designed by W. B. Knowlton of Boston and built by the Turner Construction Company. Both mills were five-story, brick and concrete structures and enclosed 850,000 square feet of floor space. They were equipped with the finest, most up-to-date machinery available in the United States and Europe. When the mills went into production in 1922–1923, they employed between 2,600 and 2,700 workers. This created certain logistical problems, which Wood, with his usual foresight, had anticipated. To provide transportation for the mill hands, the vast majority of whom lived in Lawrence, he had earlier arranged for the Boston and Maine Railroad to stop at the newly constructed Shawsheen Railroad Depot. D. L. Hardy designed and built this one-story, red-brick structure with a hipped porte-cochère roof at the entrance of the west facade. Not only did the depot accommodate the blue collar commuters, but it also enabled the white collar residents to visit Boston for a shopping spree or an evening of theatre and music. In addition to these rail facilities, Shawsheen Village was also a stop on the electrified Lawrence Division of the Eastern Massachusetts Street Railway.

To supply eating facilities for the Shawsheen Mill hands, the American Woolen Company erected a restaurant on the south side of Haverhill Street directly opposite the industrial complex. The engineering department of the firm designed the large, one-and-one-half story, red-brick building. A spacious porch with six pairs of Tuscan columns ran along the entire front of the structure. The dining area of the cafeteria could seat 800 persons. It was also equipped for the showing of motion pictures and, when the tables were removed, it could seat 1,000 spectators. In the basement was a bakery, which provided fresh bread and pastries to the cafeteria and to the Spa and Manor. The basement also contained six modern bowling alleys and locker rooms. Adjacent to the building was a red-brick dormitory for cafeteria employees. The restaurant quickly became popular with Andover residents, and the American Woolen Company opened it to the general public in July 1922. Saturday night dances were inaugurated there in early 1923.

In 1923 this self-supporting, self-contained community lacked but two essential components: a school and churches. The nineteenth-century, three-room, red-brick schoolhouse on Lowell Street was already inadequate for the 150 pupils enrolled in first through eighth grades.[30] Additionally, it was anticipated that there would be 250 grammar school age children in the village within a year.[31] Residents wanted a modern school within walking distance of their homes. After all, that was one of the great delights of living in Shaw-

Shawsheen Village School, Andover, Massachusetts. (Photograph by author)

sheen; the village was truly a walking community. Shopping, recreation, office, and transportation facilities were all within a ten-minute walk of any part of the village. Wood, in the name of the American Woolen Company, donated a five-acre plot bounded by Corbett, Poor, Magnolia, Middle, and Allen streets to the town of Andover as a site for a new school. In a special town meeting in late 1923, the citizens of Andover voted to appropriate $230,000 (the largest single appropriation to that date ever voted by the town) for the school.[32] Ripley & Le Boutillier, Boston architects, designed the two-and-one-half story building in the Georgian Revival style. The school was built in 1924 on a hill overlooking Ann Lane. Its modified Palladian windows in the southern facade were strikingly handsome.

As for the lack of religious structures in the village proper, Wood had assumed that residents would attend church services of their choice in Andover. Here were Episcopal, Methodist, Baptist, Congregational, and Roman Catholic churches. In addition, Wood permitted religious services to be conducted in the public facilities on the second floor of the Post Office building.

In tracing the genesis of this corporate community with its well-integrated residential, commercial, recreational, and industrial components, one cannot help but speculate as to the overall cost of such an undertaking. Certainly the thrifty-minded Yankees of Andover gossiped about the cost of this spectacular venture in urban planning and construction.[33] Press estimates as to the total cost of Shawsheen Village ranged from $5,000,000 to an inflated $21,000,000.[34] The exact sum will probably never be known. As late as 1928, the Town of Andover Assessor's Records carried the Shawsheen Mill complex assessment in the value of $3,604,000. These same records indicated that the 251 residential units were valued at $1,500,000.[35] The Executive Administration Building cost $2,000,000 to build and furnish. The Balmoral Spa, the Post Office, and the Merchants' Building were built at a cost of $250,000 each. All in all, actual construction and remodeling costs of this corporate community were in the neighborhood of $8,000,000. To this sum must be added the price (unknown) of the 150 acres of real estate that Wood and the American Woolen Company had purchased. For the period between 1918 and 1923, this total cost was indeed a huge expenditure.

Ownership of Shawsheen Village real estate and buildings (aside from those few original properties whose owners refused to sell) was divided between Wood himself and the American Woolen Company. The largest single piece of property in the entire village was Wood's estate Arden, which had grown to almost seventy acres by 1920. He built and owned the Post Office building, the Balmoral Spa, and the Merchants' Building. He held title to the Balmoral Playing Fields and the bowling green. He also owned several acres of gently sloping land at the southwest corner of the square, which he donated to the town of Andover as Shawsheen Park. Additionally, Wood owned the land and residential units which made up Canterbury Street (off Lowell Street). In 1921 he arranged for the creation of the Arden Trust as a legacy to his children, and all his property in the village was transferred to the trust at this time. The mill complex, the remaining commercial buildings, and the vast majority of the residential units were the property of the American Woolen Company.

Wood had intended Shawsheen Village to be a corporate community for managerial personnel. An examination of the Andover street listings for 1923 reveals that the social makeup of the residential areas was not quite what the master planner had envisioned. Most of the homes in "Brick Shawsheen" were occupied by sales managers, paymasters, overseers, superintendants, wool buyers, and other managerial personnel. "White Shawsheen," however, in addition to accountants, clerks, and bookkeepers, housed a considerable number of mill operatives, electricians, carpenters, and chauffeurs. One can only assume that the supply of housing for middle-management personnel exceeded the demand of American Woolen Company salaried help. Rather than allow the houses to remain unrented or unsold, the Homestead Association apparently accepted a wide range of renters. Even so, the middle-class makeup of the community was evident in the fact that most of the wives were listed as housewives. Only a handful of the married women in the village were employed.

Social and Civic Life

The *Andover Townsman* followed the inception and development of Wood's community with great detail. The October 3, 1919, issue carried an editorial entitled "Shawsheen Village." The final paragraph reads, "Greetings to the new Shawsheen Village! May its old and new residents keep the faith of the founders of Andover, and ever hold its record of work accomplished up to the standard being set so high by the man [William M. Wood] who is laying such wonderful foundations." Starting in July 1921, the local weekly newspaper ran a full page of Shawsheen Village news in each issue.

A perusal of the back files of the *Townsman* reveals that social and civic life in these early years was both full and varied. Tennis and bowling tournaments, winter skating parties, and bridge parties were commonplace. Amateur theatricals were popular and attracted large audiences. They were held both at the Spa and at the Casino, the large structure at the edge of the pond on the Arden estate. Cornelius Wood served as stage manager for the Shawsheen Village Dramatic Club, which was organized in early 1921. During summer months there were regular outdoor band concerts, fireworks displays on the Fourth of July, and dances at the outdoor pavilion of the Spa.

These early scenes of life in Shawsheen Village took place against the background of the Prohibition era. One can assume that a certain number of the community's residents flaunted the Twenty-eighth Amendment as casually as did a large percentage of other middle-class Americans. Evidently there was some drinking from hip flasks at the thrice-weekly outdoor dances at the Spa. Nearby residents complained of the loud noise "swearing and howling" as auto parties left the area in late evening. There were other complaints that bootleggers frequented the dances.[36] A half century later, the July 17, 1975, issue of the *Andover Townsman* carried the following bemused account of those "raucous dances":

> The selectmen, at a special meeting on Monday morning, 50 years ago this week, granted a license to the Shawsheen Pharmacy, Inc., to conduct two dancing parties per week in Balmoral Gardens not to "exceed the hour of 11 p.m., no minors under 17 admitted, and grounds policed at expense of licensee after the dance in order that there be no loitering. . . .
>
> In deference to the residents of Shawsheen Village, who have complained about the noise and quality of the music, the sounding board must be faced toward the east."

Arthur M. Schlesinger, Sr., noted American historian, long ago observed that Americans are a nation of joiners. The early residents of Shawsheen Village certainly bear out his generalization. The Shawsheen Women's Club was founded in October 1921 (and continues today to be an active organization); the club sponsored a variety of activities such as lectures, musicals, and tours. Mrs. William M. Wood, Sr. and Mrs. Cornelius A. Wood were charter members of the club.

The Shawsheen Village Improvement Society was established in February 1921. It was founded by Cornelius A. Wood, George M. Wallace, Ignatius McNulty, and Dr. George Wallace to promote the general welfare of the growing community.[37] This group was instrumental in securing the assignment of an Andover police officer to direct traffic in the village square. The policeman's elevated shelter is visible in early photos of the square. The organization also inaugurated the movement to call for the construction of a modern elementary school in the village. In addition, the Shawsheen Village Improvement Society approved all articles to be considered at the semi-annual village meetings, which began in March 1921. Another organization designed to benefit the community was the Shawsheen Cooperative Bank, which opened for business on February 1, 1924. Cornelius A. Wood was a member of the board of directors. The bank's main function was to provide mortgage loans for residents.

Inasmuch as most of the villagers were married couples—many of them young—children played an important role in the community's life. A kindergarten was established, a local Parent-Teacher Association chapter was formed in early 1922, and a children's playground opened on the Balmoral Playing Fields. Punch-and-Judy shows and supervised swimming in Hussey's Pond were but two of a variety of activities geared to the youngsters. As previously mentioned, Shawsheen Village boasted its own Boys' Club building, which was home to the local Boy Scout troop.

In 1923 *The Town Crier*, the first directory of Shawsheen Village was published.[38] The twenty-six-page booklet listed the business firms in the commercial district, train and electric trolley schedules, and the locations of the seven fire alarm boxes in the village. It also included a listing of all the newly laid out streets and a brief sketch of the development of the community. Apropos of railroad and electric trolley schedules, only secondarily did the village residents depend upon railroad and trolley service. Wood's corporate community was geared to the automobile.

As might be expected, Shawsheen Village attracted scores of visitors. The Boston press gave considerable illustrated coverage to this experiment in urban planning. Both the Spa and the Shawsheen Manor were popular stops for Sunday auto parties from as far away as Manchester, New Hampshire, and Worcester, Massachusetts. The Manor, which had a German chef, quickly

William M. Wood, holding a cane (front row), with American Woolen Company executives, on steps of the Casino, Arden, Andover, Massachusetts. (*Booster*, July, 1921. Courtesy of Lawrence Public Library)

earned high marks for its cuisine and gracious service. In 1921 one could order a complete lobster dinner for two dollars. The guest register of the Manor listed Madame Galli-Curci, famed Italian opera diva, in May 1923, and Sir Harry Lauder, well-known Scottish singer and composer, in February 1924. Although the Prince of Wales did not stay at the Manor during his trip to Shawsheen Village on October 23, 1924, most villagers turned out to cheer as the royal motorcade drove through the community. The Union Jack was prominently displayed as the crowd waved to the future King Edward VIII.[39]

Post card views of Shawsheen Village quickly became fast selling items at the Spa. There were photos of Arden, Orlando Cottage, residential dwellings, the Spa, the Administration Building, the Merchants' Building, the Balmoral Playing Fields, the Shawsheen River with its canoes and rowboats, Hussey's Pond, the village garage, and the bowling green. Today, a Shawsheen Village postal cancellation on the rare one-cent George Washington stamp has become a collector's item.

William Wood often hosted large gatherings of American Woolen Company officials and their families at Arden. On June 25, 1920, thirteen special railroad coaches brought 2,000 company employees who were under the age of twenty to Shawsheen for an afternoon outing. Mr. Wood, his daughter

Balmoral Spa, Shawsheen Village, Andover, Massachusetts, September 10, 1921.
The decorations were in honor of Wood's return from a European tour.
(*Booster*, October, 1921. Courtesy of Lawrence Public Library)

Rosalind, Mr. and Mrs. William M. Wood, Jr., and Mr. and Mrs. Cornelius A. Wood greeted their guests. Besides the luncheon, which was served in two large tents, there was a program of boxing and wrestling matches, a concert, and community singing. A third mammoth tent covered an outdoor dance pavilion where a jazz orchestra played tunes for dancing. Less than three weeks later, the Woods hosted still another picnic reception. On July 15, 1920, special trains brought 2,000 agents, overseers, and their families to Shawsheen Village. A huge, gaily colored tent was the scene of a luncheon that included bouillon, chicken and lobster salad, light pastries, ices, and lemonade. There was a jazz band for dancing.

Saturday, September 10, 1921, was perhaps the most festive day ever in these early years of Shawsheen Village. The villagers held a special welcome home celebration for William Wood, who had spent much of the summer in England, France, and Germany. His private train arrived at the newly completed Shawsheen Village Railway Depot shortly after noon. As he stepped from his Pullman car, a band played "For He's A Jolly Good Fellow"; practically every resident of the village joined in the chorus. Mr. Wood's motorcade, followed by a crowd of 400, proceeded slowly to the square. Flags, bunting, and banners covered every building along the way. At the square,

Mr. and Mrs. William M. Wood on the Bowling Green, Shawsheen Village, Andover, Massachusetts, September 10, 1921. (*Booster*, October, 1921. Courtesy of Lawrence Public Library)

the president of the American Woolen Company officially opened the bowling green by bowling the first ball to start the play on the three rinks. Then he moved on to watch tennis tournaments and a soccer match between the American Woolen and the Lowell Cotton teams. Then followed a folk dance exhibition on the lawn of the Shawsheen Manor by the children from the Boxford Camp. The chorus of the Shawsheen Village Girls' Club also presented a musical program. At 6:00 P.M. Mr. Wood was honored at a dinner for 200 in the Manor. It is not known if he then journeyed across the square to the Spa for the regular Saturday night dance. He must have been moved by this display of affection from so many of his neighbors and "fellow workers" in Shawsheen Village and pleased by the apparent success of his plans.

This potpourri of social doings in Shawsheen Village in the early 1920s suggests a country club atmosphere. The very concept of a crime rate for this model community was both unthinkable and without basis in fact. Had F. Scott Fitzgerald lived here, it might well have been the setting for his *This*

Side of Paradise (1920) or *The Great Gatsby* (1925). Indeed, by 1925 the village was a miniature version of an exclusive, upper-middle-class American suburb. William Wood's dream had turned into reality.

Initially, however, Wood's project did not meet with universal approval from the citizens of Andover. In large measure the townspeople welcomed and admired the new addition, but there were occasional caveats. Some Andoverians did not like anything about Wood.[40] Old-timers resented the name change from Frye Village to Shawsheen Village. This resentment resurfaced from time to time, as in March of 1924 when Wood's request to change the name of Poor Street to Oxford Street was voted down in a town meeting.[41] Others feared that Wood wanted to make the village a part of Lawrence. Wood wrote to the *Andover Townsman* on December 14, 1923, to assure the local community that he opposed annexation of Shawsheen Village to Lawrence. "The new residents are delighted to belong to Andover," he commented.

There were dire warnings from some of the citizens that Wood's experiment would cost the town's taxpayers dearly. Actually, Shawsheen Village from the very beginning of its development through 1922 was more than self-supporting, and it was during these years that most of the construction took place. Town expenditures for sewerage, street and bridge construction, and municipal services in Shawsheen Village in these years totalled $71,595, some $14,000 *less* than tax revenues from William Wood and the American Woolen Company for the same period. With the exception of the construction of the Shawsheen School in 1923, the Town of Andover has not expended a single major sum in the village this past half-century.

Some Andoverians took offense at what they considered the "snobbishness" of the early residents of Shawsheen Village. A large number of these American Woolen Company officials and junior executives earned considerable salaries and operated expensive motor vehicles. Many of them had domestic help in their homes. Because of the self-contained nature of the community, residents of Shawsheen rarely mixed with townspeople from "up the hill." This social aloofness was apparently shared by school-aged children of the village. "They thought they were better than the rest of us," an older resident of Andover once observed to this writer. Gradually, as newcomers attracted by the charm and beauty of the village replaced many of the original residents, this seeming aloofness disappeared.

There was no doubt that the community was both beautiful and charming. D. M. Scott's poem "Shawsheen Village," which was published in the *Andover Townsman* on February 9, 1923 attributed this attractiveness to the genius of one man:

Like a sunrise in summer, so fair to be seen
Rose the Queen of the Valley, bonnie Shawsheen
With its streets and its homes all modern and grand
And its buildings the peer of any in the land
Each forming a part of a wonderful plan
That was born in the brain of a remarkable man
A prince of industry of national fame
Who in building Shawsheen adds lustre to his name.

The poet was not the only one to give credit where credit was due. Most of the people of Andover shared the view of Claude M. Fuess, distinguished headmaster of Phillips Academy, when he wrote in 1959 in *Andover: Symbol of New England:* "To William M. Wood and Thomas Cochran [wealthy Phillips Academy alumnus and trustee who gave some $11,000,000 to that school's building program in the 1920s] our town owes much of its present charm. It is more beautiful because they were generous and imaginative."[42]

But the generosity and imagination that Wood had poured into the creation of Shawsheen Village in the years from 1918 to 1923 would soon be questioned and criticized by the directors and officials of the American Woolen Company. His triumphant business career was about to crash down upon him.

CHAPTER VI

Wood's Final Years: Triumphs Beget Tragedies

Dᴜʀɪɴɢ the early months of the building of Shawsheen Village, William Wood stood at the pinnacle of his career. He was sixty-two years of age, and his energy and physical constitution seemed undiminished. The same could be said of his giant textile firm. Seldom in American business history "has any company that profited from an entry into war been able to profit almost equally from the onset of peace."[1] Never had American Woolen's corporate cheek—nor Wood's—been so brightly flushed with profits than in the years from 1916 through 1923.

Capitalization was increased by $20,000,000 in 1920 and by another $10,000,000 in 1923. By the latter year the original 1899 capitalization of some $45,000,000 had been doubled. The value of the firm's preferred stock climbed to an all-time high of $169.50 a share in 1919. Business journals, intoxicated by the very size of Wood's firm, customarily referred to American Woolen as an "empire"; to the emperor such talk appeared not at all displeasing.[2] In his report of 1923, the president proudly announced that the firm was again expanding.

> Believing in the steady growth of the consumptive power of the country and advantageous opportunities having been presented the company acquired the Strathmore Worsted Mills of Concord, Massachusetts, the Tilton Mills of Tilton, New Hampshire, the Black River Mills of Ludlow, Vermont, and the S. Slater &

Sons Woolen Mills of Webster, Massachusetts. The last named, which is by far the most important acquisition, has been renamed the Webster Mill and will be improved and extended. . . . *The management is prepared for any eventuality and looks forward to 1924 with full confidence . . .*" (italics added).[3]

By 1924 the corporation employed 40,000 workers and consisted of sixty mills scattered throughout eight states. (See Appendix A.) Book assets totalled $150,000,000 and the gross business in 1924 was $175,000,000. In that year, the American Woolen Company produced a total output of all classes of fabrics of some seventy million yards. This figure equals a web of cloth approximately forty thousand miles in length, almost sufficient to twice encircle the globe.[4] Yet in 1924 the American Woolen Company lost a staggering $6,900,000. "On the advice of his physician," Wood resigned the presidency in late December 1924.

What had happened? There are few examples in American industry of such a sudden transition from profit to loss. That this occurred during a period of increasing general prosperity is even more unusual.

The American Woolen Company was organized on the theory that size gave volume and volume gave profits. "It was a simple arithmetical formula— you got your 'share' of the total business and you made your 'share' of the total profits. There was no emphasis on individual superiority in manufacturing or in salesmanship."[5] It was a successful enough formula for its day. But by the early 1920s the markets had changed and the formula collapsed.

From 1916 through 1923, Wood had been the dominating giant of a vast seller's market. When the field reversed itself in the mid-1920s and became a buyer's market, he was totally unprepared to cope with this new reality. As *Fortune* magazine succinctly summarized it in March 1954, "Symbolically, the uniform-cloth business was done to death by the flapper and the plus-four; for clothes became fewer, lighter in weight, fancier in fabric, and less likely to be made of wool."

Throughout the history of the modern woolen industry only two methods of woolen merchandising have succeeded in a big way: (1) to start at the top of the price range and dominate the market by creative weaving and dyeing; (2) to remain at the bottom of the price range and sell nothing but staples in huge quantities.[6] Wood, during his presidency, dominated the latter field. When he first formed his company, the whole industry waited with bated breath for his quotation on blue serge. With his great production facilities and cost accounting statistics, "whatever his price, it represented the least that could be added to raw material [costs] by its manufacture into clothing goods."[7] Blue serge was the bread and butter of the American Woolen

Company. Together with one or two other sturdy staples, it was made in tremendous quantities, particularly by the larger mills. Under Wood's control, the firm relied upon mass production in the low-priced field. It was apparently satisfied to make something just as good as the fellow down the river did. With the great production capacity of its 10,000 looms, which in 1923 comprised one-sixth of the nation's 64,000 woolen looms, the company dominated the field of staple woolen fabrics.[8] The end was signaled in late 1923 with the sharp decline in blue serge demand. The $6,500,000 net that Wood's firm made that year was its last significant profit (save for a lucky inventory windfall in 1933) until World War II and the Korean War created a new market for woolen uniforms.

As one examines the sixty-mill combination that Wood assembled, its reputation as an "empire" seems somewhat exaggerated. The Shawsheen Village mills, not completed until 1923, were the only new factories in this collection of old or aging enormous New England mills. Their very size and number betrayed the American Woolen Company for what it was—a mass producer of staples floundering in an age of style. Until the very end of his career, however, Wood continued to follow his philosophy of mergers and growth. The very size of the firm was what had produced the enormous profits of the war and early-post-war years. There were occasional omens of the difficulties ahead, but he apparently ignored them. For example, in 1921 the company's export subsidiary was liquidated. His dream of clothing naked Europe ran afoul of European textile manufacturers who quickly went back into production in 1919 and 1920.[9] Convinced of the infallibility of his philosophy, Wood plunged into further expansion in 1923. This obsession with "bigger is better" and more profitable proved to be his downfall in 1924.

Another apparent weakness in the American Woolen Company was in its organizational structure. Executive offices were located in Boston and sales offices in Manhattan. Contact between the various mills and the sales force was frequently direct, which often resulted in poor coordination between sales and management.[10] The great size of the firm had, by the 1920s, made Wood's innovative organizational system ineffective.

Still other problems beset William Wood and the company in these years. A major mistake in financing occurred in 1920 when Wood ordered the sale of $20,000,000 additional common stock. The flotation of this stock by the underwriting syndicate came right at the time of a severe financial crisis. "Not until the middle of 1922 did the market price of this security recover to a point equal to that when the flotation was essayed."[11] Wood's skills seemed to be slipping.

As early as 1920, friends and associates noted that Wood's "sudden bold moves were less uniformly brilliant."[12] Indeed, some of them appeared eccentric, particularly Shawsheen Village. Part of this change could be attributed to family problems. The death of his mother in 1916 greatly upset him. He buried her in his family plot in West Parish Cemetery and arranged to have the body of his father moved from the Catholic Burial Grounds in New Bedford so that his parents might rest side by side. In 1918 the sudden death of his youngest child, Irene, at the age of twenty-four further unnerved him. For months after her funeral, he would frequently get into a horse-drawn buggy and drive to her grave site. There, for long hours he would sit grieving in solitude. Because Irene had been particularly fond of animals, he erected a granite water trough in her memory in Shawsheen Square.

In late 1919 another family matter must surely have hurt and disappointed the elder Wood. William Jr. announced that he did not want to succeed his father as president. "Bill did not like the jealousies that exist in a big company," his brother later wrote.[13] The long-cherished dream of William Wood was not to be. His elder son resigned the vice-presidency and went into partnership with Frederick R. Edington in a wool merchandising business. William Jr. became the president of Edington and Company.

Family problems were not the only source of trouble, however. In the spring of 1920, William Wood had his second serious brush with the law. Years earlier in 1913, a Boston jury had acquitted him of charges that he had been implicated in the "dynamite plot" of the 1912 Lawrence strike. The 1920 legal case came about after United States Attorney General A. Mitchell Palmer instituted criminal proceedings against the American Woolen Company and Wood for violating the Lever Act. This 1917 law, effective for the duration of the war, was a broad-sweeping measure. One of its goals was to prevent excessive profiteering. Wood and his firm were accused of making excessive profits in the manufacture and sale of wearing apparel. Wood's attorney was Charles Evans Hughes, unsuccessful Republican presidential candidate in 1916. Judge Julian N. Mack presided over the trial, which took place in the United States District Court in New York City on Friday, June 11, 1920. Hughes demurred to the indictment on the grounds that woolen cloth was not wearing apparel and that the sale of woolen cloth did not violate the law. The bench sustained the demurrer and quashed the indictment.[14] That evening, several thousand American Woolen Company mill operatives from Lawrence assembled behind a banner reading "A Man Without A Stain Upon His Honor" and marched to Arden. Wood and his two sons thanked the demonstrators.[15]

116

By 1921, Wood's three surviving children had reached adulthood. Indeed, his two sons were both married and had children. With this in mind, the elder Wood and his wife established the Arden Trust on February 9, 1921. The three children were named the sole beneficiaries and the elder Wood was appointed sole trustee. The value of the initial gift, mostly in Shawsheen Village real estate, was $1,163,472. On October 8, 1921, Wood added American Woolen Company stock and other securities valued in excess of $1,200,000. By June 1924 he had added still more, and the total value of the Arden Trust was $3,211,510. Wood often expressed the belief "that his children should have funds of their own in order that they might learn to handle money, and prepare themselves for the lives that they would lead as children of a wealthy man."[16]

William Madison Wood was indeed a wealthy man. His federal income tax for 1918, which the American Woolen Company paid, was $681,169. His salary and commissions for that year was $978,725.[17] It is worth recalling that this was a war year and taxes on large incomes were extremely heavy. Wood's net worth, as it appeared on his books, varied between 1915 and 1925, "but at no time during this period was he worth less than $2,967,788, nor more than $5,000,000."[18]

Wood's robust health began to fail him in 1922. Early that year, he had an attack of Bell's palsy which manifested itself in a slight and temporary paralysis of the muscles in his left cheek. He also had put on considerable weight. In addition to these physical ailments, there came a blow on the afternoon of August 15, 1922, from which he never fully recovered. William M. Wood, Jr. and a friend, Major Alexander Gardner, were instantly killed when Wood's Rolls Royce sedan crashed into a telephone pole on the North Reading-Andover road. The elder Wood sped to the scene of the accident where, according to eye-witnesses, his grief was painful to behold.[19] "Dad was never the same again. He remained oppressed with sorrow," Cornelius Wood later recalled.[20] Not even the completion of Shawsheen Village could take his mind off the tragic death of his namesake. The youth had been so involved in the conception and execution of this model corporate community that the village became a daily reminder to the father of his loss. Despondency now affected his mind. "His temper became uncontrollable," wrote his younger son. "He muttered ominously to himself."[21]

Somehow, the family apparently managed to hide Wood's deteriorating mental condition from the business world and the general public. Occasionally there were still flashes of his genius as an industrialist and financier. In late 1922 he played a prominent part in the reorganization of the Consolidated

Textile Company of New York City. He was elected director-general and chairman of the board. This reorganization and the entrance of Wood on the board "was hailed at the time as the largest woolen and cotton combine in the history of the industry."[22] In his final years, Wood had scored still another first. But it was to be his last Wall Street coup. By early 1924 he had lost control of the American Woolen Company.

How this came about is not fully known, but there are enough bits of circumstantial evidence to form a scenario. Some time after World War I, Wood decided to cash in a large part of his holdings in American Woolen Company securities. He consulted with his sons. Cornelius advised that "to retain the presidency, this control could be important. . . . However, Dad felt that no one else could run the company. . . ."[23] Wood felt that he could take the risk, that no management could get along without him. He arranged with Brown Brothers, bankers, to buy his stock. With Wood's customary financial acumen, he undoubtedly made his transaction when American Woolen Company stock was selling at a high price.

Although this was a sound financial decision—as time would reveal—it opened the door to trouble from certain stockholders.[24] Cornelius Wood's autobiography is replete with tales of jealous executives looking out for themselves, of plots and counter-plots.[25] A powerful group of new investors wanted a complete change in management.[26] The Boston and New York press alleged "there have been frequently recurring demands for Wood's official head."[27] It was only a matter of time before they got their wish.

While vacationing in Havana, Cuba, in the spring of 1924, Wood had a mild stroke; but rumors of his impending resignation were vehemently denied by members of the Wood family.[28] A second stroke occurred in the summer of that year and left him with a pronounced limp in his left leg. On August 9, 1924, while he was recovering from this ailment, a bronze, recessed bust—the gift of the employees of the American Woolen Company—was unveiled in the main lobby of the Executive Administration Building in Shawsheen Village. Wood was too ill to attend the ceremony.[29]

In late December 1924, Dr. Arthur G. Griffin, his personal physician, gave his patient a simple choice: "Resign or die." Cornelius Wood, who was present when his father resigned on December 31, 1924, penned a brief but moving account of the scene.

> Thinking only of his welfare, his family and loyal friends, joined by those not so loyal, persuaded Dad to resign. The meeting where he did so was a sad one. The badly shaken old man seated on the couch in the living room at "Arden" took a pen in hand and affixed his signature to the papers. . . . This signature bore but

faint semblance to the once decisive "William M. Wood" we were accustomed to seeing.[30]

At this meeting Wood appointed Andrew G. Pierce, Jr. to succeed him in the presidency and named Cornelius Wood as first vice-president.[31] With his faltering hand, the sixty-eight-year-old Wood thus terminated his nineteen-year presidency of the American Woolen Company.

Now broken in both mind and body, he had to suffer still another cruel blow. "With his resignation in hand they [his critics and enemies] smashed his pet project [Shawsheen Village]," a sympathetic writer later commented in the *Boston Post*.[32] In early 1925, President Pierce, son of the man who had given Wood his first job in the textile industry, ordered the closing of the Executive Administration Building in Shawsheen Village. The company's exodus from the model community began almost immediately.

Without Wood's controlling hand, the demise of his corporate community seemed to be a *fait accompli*. Many officials of the American Woolen Company had viewed the creation of the village as a "fool scheme."[33] They worried about the cost of this grandiose experiment. Once they got their hands on the company books, they were aghast at the amount of money that Wood had poured into his dream. There had been danger signals. When Wood directed the relocation of the executive and managerial staff from Boston to Shawsheen Village in the spring of 1923, there were scattered grumblings and a few flat refusals to comply.[34] Since "Mr. Wood's will was American Woolen's law," as *Fortune* magazine commented in June 1935, by the early fall of 1923 the huge building hummed with activity. Yet the resentment apparently remained.

If one shares the view that the creation of Shawsheen Village was another foible of an eccentric millionaire, then the most serious psychological mistakes that Wood made in building this multi-million dollar community can be forgiven. Apparently it never entered his mind that people who work together do not necessarily want to live, recreate, and socialize together, and certainly not in a community built within view of the master's hill-top mansion. Among many of the new residents of the village "there was a great clamor to move out."[35] Actually, there was something almost feudal about the whole scheme; the lord of the manor with his happy nobility living and working beneath his watchful eye. Wood's dream was doomed by the very egocentricity of the man. He never realized that he could not assemble and direct peoples' lives as he assembled mills and dominated the American Woolen Company.

Wood, at least, was spared the hurt and pain of actually seeing the end of his dream. He was on one of his European vacations—this time for health—when he read of Pierce's decision to abandon Shawsheen Village as headquarters of the corporation. While he attempted to regain his health in Europe, stockholders were busily engaged in criticizing his management. Their special ire was directed at Shawsheen Village.[36]

Shortly after this, Cornelius Wood, who had made an unsuccessful bid to win the presidency of the firm, resigned.[37] Later, he penned the following lines in his autobiography:

> With Dad's resignation and then mine, an era was closed in which the name of Wood was paramount in the woolen industry; and thus the Woods were forever severed from the American Woolen Company in particular and the industry in general. The breakup of William M. Wood also spelled the beginning of the end of the largest wool manufacturing enterprise the world has known.[38]

The "breakup" of William Madison Wood also heralded the end of a remarkable industrial statesman. On the morning of February 2, 1926, he took his own life along a lonely, sandy road in Daytona, Florida.

Wood's behavior in the final, tragic months of his life was at times irrational. He had the hallucination that he was "too poor to travel anymore."[39] In the fall of 1925 he directed his private secretary, George M. Wallace, to sell The Towers, his mansion in Palm Beach, because the climate was too warm.[40] The family took a $300,000 loss on the sale.[41] On another occasion, a person who hoped to become Wood's beneficiary convinced him to omit Cornelius from his will. The younger Wood had a confrontation with his father and was reinstated as principal benefactor and executor.[42]

In early January 1926, Mr. and Mrs. Wood, who had been a semi-invalid for several years, traveled south for the winter, accompanied by Dr. Griffin, a chauffeur, a valet, a nurse, and a maid. The party stayed at the Hotel Ormond in Daytona, Florida. For several days prior to his suicide, Wood remarked repeatedly to his physician "I'd be better off dead" and "life isn't worth living." Knowing Wood's depressed mental state, it seems surprising that Dr. Griffin did not take him seriously.[43] That Wood sometimes carried a revolver was common knowledge.

On the morning of February 2nd, Wood ordered his limousine. Accompanied only by his valet, Augustine Frederickson, and his chauffeur, Joseph A. Beaulieu, he drove to an unfrequented stretch of highway. Directing his servants to remain in the car, he walked around a curve in the road. He placed a .38-calibre revolver in his mouth and pulled the trigger.

His health ruined, his spectacular business career abruptly terminated, Irene and Billy "taken from me," his dream of Shawsheen Village now bitter

120

ashes, his mind distraught, even unbalanced, William Wood apparently saw no reason for living as he walked along the lonely road that seemed to lead nowhere. As might be expected, Wood's suicide made the front pages of much of the nation's press.[44] Residents of Andover and Shawsheen Village were stunned by the news. His body was returned to his beloved Arden. On February 8, 1926, in the aftermath of a blizzard, he was buried at the side of his parents and his two children.

In death as in life, Wood remains something of an enigma. His was a complex personality, with seemingly contradictory elements. Yet it is clear that the desire to succeed was *the* motivating force in his life. An American-born-and-bred child, he was, nonetheless, the son of a Portuguese father and a mother of mixed Portuguese-English descent. As with many a Portuguese mariner, Wood's father abandoned his surname upon arrival in America and adopted an Anglo-Saxon surname. His original Portuguese name still cannot be ascertained. Wood's parents were probably Roman Catholic by birth, but there is little indication they actually practiced their faith except for an occasional baptism. These facts suggest that the young immigrant couple, like many others in this period, wanted to downplay their true heritage in order to become Americans. Their son apparently wanted to do the same thing, except that he evidently desired more than just being an American. He wanted to be among those in the highest echelons of society. Growing up in the decades following the Civil War, Wood must have wholeheartedly believed in the "American Gospel of Success," and craved the fame, money, and power that success offered. To obtain them, it was said, all he had to do was follow the formulas provided by the Horatio Algers and the Phineas Barnums. Yet for Wood to be accepted among the business and social elite, he also had to overcome the obstacle of his heritage. This need is interwoven through most of his extraordinary rags-to-riches career.

Upon the death of his father, he plunged into the Yankee New Bedford world of work. His keen mind, driving ambition, and love of work eventually won him acceptance and advancement in the industrial circles of the city. His early association with the Yankee masters of this New England textile city profoundly impressed him. Years later he recalled "their splendid character and honor." "I regarded . . . [these men] as something superhuman, and looked upon them with awe and wonder."[45]

Following his marriage to Ellen Wheaton Ayer in 1888, when he was thirty years of age, Wood appears to have thrown himself whole-heartedly into the world of Yankeedom. He became an Episcopalian and a Republican. He joined exclusive Yankee social clubs and sent his sons to private preparatory schools where they associated with the Astors, the Choates, the Rhein-landers, and others from society's upper crust. He staffed the American Woolen Company with Yankee underlings. His favorite estate, Arden, was in Andover, Massachusetts, the "Symbol of New England." As Marcus L. Hansen, the eminent Harvard historian, long ago observed, "Nothing was more Yankee than a Yankeeized person of foreign descent."[46]

By 1900, so complete was his transformation from being the son of humble Portuguese immigrant parents to being a Yankee capitalist that he informed the federal census enumerator that his father had been born in Scotland. He listed his mother's place of birth as Madeira, a Portuguese island off the coast of Morocco, famed as a British resort area. One can only assume that he was anxious to remove this last Portuguese trace from his adopted Yankee world.

Apropos of William Wood's 1900 attempt to eradicate his Portuguese heritage, his mother apparently attempted to do the same for herself. In 1900 she informed the census taker that she was born in Massachusetts and that both of her parents were born in England. Wood's surviving sisters, Emma and Susan, and his brother Otis also reported that their parents, William Jason and Amelia Christiana Wood, were born in Massachusetts. Yet, the birth certificates of William, Susan, Otis, and Emma indicate that their parents were born on Pico in the Azores. Likewise, Amelia Christiana Madison Wood's death certificate states that she was born in the Azores. It would appear that by 1900, the members of the Wood family did not bother to check with one another as to exactly what their roots were or were to be reported.

Another related facet of Wood's many-sided personality, was his patriotism; perhaps Americanism is a more apt term. Much of his fervor can be attributed to the fact that his lifetime encompassed three periods of intense national patriotism caused by the United States' involvement in wars. Yet Wood appears almost to flaunt his Americanism in his later years. The Americanization program that he instituted in the American Woolen Company in the years following World War I was typical. As with other industrial leaders who employed large numbers of immigrants, Wood wanted his employees to learn the English language and adopt American customs and ideals. He apparently believed, as did most men like him, that if his workers became Americanized, they would be less likely to follow the advice of radical labor agitators, whom Wood frequently described as "foreigners." In the aftermath of the Lawrence strike of 1912, Wood supported the Reverend James O'Reilly's drive for a "God and Country" parade in Lawrence. More than likely, Wood financed the purchase of the over 30,000 American flags that were carried by the paraders on Columbus Day, 1912.[47]

"For God and Country Parade," Columbus Day, 1912, Lawrence, Massachusetts. (Courtesy of Merrimack Valley Textile Museum)

During the "Red Scare" of 1919, Wood's anti-I. W. W. and anti-Bolshevik statements angered radicals throughout the nation. In late April 1919, United States postal authorities in New York City intercepted thirty-eight bombs (in identical packages) addressed to some of the most prominent leaders in the nation. Among the intended recipients were John D. Rockefeller, J. P. Morgan, Associate Justice Oliver Wendell Holmes, Attorney General A. Mitchell Palmer, and William M. Wood.[48]

Personally, Wood seems to have relished identifying with American history. The Colonial Revival design of the residential houses in Shawsheen Village is one of many examples. The American eagle and the Shawsheen Indian were—aside from the ram's head, symbol of the American Woolen Company—his favorite motifs. It was Wood who had selected the firm's name back in 1899. He also built the so-called replica of George Washington's Valley Forge headquarters in his corporate community. And from the top of the 120-foot flagpole at his estate on Cuttyhunk, the Stars and Stripes usually waved. Perhaps all this was but another side of his Yankeeism.

So numerous are the paradoxes of William Wood's character that they make most generalizations difficult. He was vain yet self-effacing. At a time when he was one of the highest salaried executives in the United States, he casually remarked to reporters who quizzed him about his four-dollar a week salary in the early 1870s, ". . . I was overpaid then as I have always been since."[49] He was arrogant yet thoughtful. He could be ruthless with those who crossed him, yet he could also be forgiving. He was autocratic, yet he liked to refer to his 40,000 employees as "my fellow workers." He was intensely private yet usually was in the public eye. Supremely self-confident, he nonetheless craved adulation. Shrewdly cost conscious in business dealings, he was generous to a fault in his personal life.

Perhaps only a psycho-historian could adequately explain his mania for mills, mergers, and mansions. Clearly, they represented an overwhelming need for power. It has often been observed that the thirst for power feeds upon itself. Wood's life seems no exception to this generalization. All the triumphs of his long, spectacular business career ended in personal tragedy.

One is again tempted to draw a parallel between the remarkable lives of William Wood and Andrew Carnegie. Both were the sons of poor immigrant parents who had come to America within eight years of one another; the Carnegies from Scotland, the Woods from the Azores. Both boys had started their Horatio Alger-like careers in the textile industry; Carnegie in Pittsburgh, Pennsylvania, in 1848, Wood, in New Bedford, Massachusetts, in 1870. Their starting wages gave little hint of the wealth and power the two men would one day wield. Carnegie, the greatest iron and steel manufacturer of the nineteenth century, was the richest man in the world by 1901. It was his firm that formed the nucleus of the United States Steel Corporation, which J. P. Morgan organized in that year. Two years earlier, in 1899, Wood master-minded the world's first multi-million dollar woolen corporation, the American Woolen Company.

For the next quarter-century, Wood devoted his considerable abilities and tireless energies to satisfying his insatiable desire for more mills and mergers for his corporation, and more luxuries and mansions for his family. In contrast, Carnegie spent most of these same years in giving away his great fortune. Additionally, his interests and activities ranged from industry to politics, education, pacifism, and philanthropy. The Napoleon of the woolen industry, on the other hand, had but two interests, his family and his firm. Carnegie and Wood were impulsive, haughty, autocratic and shrewd. Yet, both could be compassionate and warm human beings. During the course of their long business careers, each of them appeared at their worst in dealing with labor unrest: Carnegie with the tragic Homestead strike of 1892 and Wood with the bitter Lawrence strike of 1912.

In 1889, Carnegie penned a remarkable social essay entitled "Wealth." The thesis of his gospel of wealth was simply stated: "The problem of our age is the proper administration of wealth." To Carnegie there appeared only three alternatives by which a man of great wealth could dispose of his fortune: he could leave it to his family, he could bequeath it in his will for public purposes, or he could administer it during his own lifetime for public benefits. "Of the three, the least desirable both for society and for the individual was the first. . . . The thoughtful man must . . . say, 'I would as soon leave to my son a curse as the almighty dollar', and admit to himself that it is not the welfare of the children, but family pride, which inspires these legacies."[50]

Although Wood's wealth was minute in comparison with Carnegie's hundreds of millions of dollars, at the time of his death, Wood's personal estate was valued at $4,750,911.[51] Perhaps Wood had never heard of Carnegie's maxim: "The man who dies thus rich, dies disgraced." The bulk of Wood's fortune went to his children.

"American Woolen—The Greatest Name In Woolens" was the motto of the firm that he had created. Perhaps a fitting epitaph for this remarkable industrialist might be: "William Madison Wood—the greatest name in the history of woolen manufacturing."

1947 aerial view of Shawsheen Village, Andover, Massachusetts.
Arden, the Wood estate, lower left corner of photograph.
(Courtesy of Andover Historical Society)

126

CHAPTER VII

Afterword

For a quarter of a century from 1899 to 1924, Wood had orchestrated and directed every movement of the American Woolen Company. There was never any doubt that it was his show.[1] And there was no one in the organization who was trained to replace him. Without his firm and guiding hand after 1924, American Woolen drifted about like a great ship in the Sargasso Sea. Andrew G. Pierce, Jr. was an able successor, but, incredible as it may sound, he attempted to run the company on a part-time basis. He was still deeply involved with his family-owned New Bedford Mills and devoted only three days a week to American Woolen affairs.[2] His primary effort seems to have been a salvage operation.

Pierce sold three plants, closed twenty-seven others, and concentrated production "in the remaining more efficient mills" (an oft-repeated phrase in the post-Wood era of the company's history).[3] He also reduced inventories of raw material and finished goods. These retrenchment measures were not enough, however. There was a deficit of $4,225,000 for 1926; in 1928, another deficit of $1,260,000; and still another deficit in 1929, this one in the amount of $4,228,000. Wood's mighty empire was crumbling.

Pierce's annual reports attempted to allay fears, but by 1929, the 20,000 stockholders (there were 800,000 shares of common and preferred stock outstanding) were restless. No common dividend had been paid since 1924. Not even the preferred stock had returned a single penny to its holders since the second quarter of 1927. The absence of dividends was due to outstanding bank loans in the amount of $11,000,000. These included $5,500,000 that Wood had borrowed to finance the cost of Shawsheen Village and $5,500,000 that he had borrowed to purchase the Webster Mills in 1923. By sacrificing dividends, Pierce managed to pay off the indebtedness and to increase cash reserves by $13,000,000.[4] Such Draconian measures, however, played havoc with Wall Street trading. The firm's 1923 preferred high of 111¾ plunged to a 1929 low of 15½. Common stock fared even worse. Its 1923 high of 109⅝ sagged to a low of 5⅞ for 1929. As more American Woolen Company stock was dumped by dissatisfied shareholders, the buyer's market kept bidding low.

The American Woolen Company never had accumulated a large funded debt, so it frequently found itself knocking at the collective doors of its bankers (Brown Brothers, Chase National, and Hayden, Stone) for short-term loans. Irked by the constant deficits, the bankers got together and bought a large block of American Woolen stock on the open market. Slowly they infiltrated the board of directors. In February 1931 they made their move for control of the company.[5] Pierce resigned as chairman of the board, and the bankers replaced him with William B. Warner, successful president of the McCall Corporation, publisher of women's magazines. Lionel J. Noah, merchandising manager of Gimbel's department store in Philadelphia was named president. The bankers pinned their hopes on these known masters of style and fashion to rebuild their firm. Both Noah and Warner were out to give the public what it wanted instead of what they thought the public ought to have. They closed the Boston executive offices and moved company headquarters to Manhattan. For the first time in the history of the firm, sales and production chieftains were under one roof.

The new directors created the Textile Realty Company, which proceeded to sell many of the mills that Pierce had closed at bankrupt prices. Between 1931 and 1935, twenty-one mills were sold. Two of the mills with an assessed valuation of $100,000 were sold for $4,300. As *Fortune* magazine commented, "whatever the tax assessor may have thought them worth, their value to American Woolen was zero minus overhead."[6]

Somehow the firm continued to stagger along. The more than $100,000,000 in profits that it had made during the Wood years apparently provided "enough fat to sustain it for decades."[7] But the drain was steady and ominous. From 1924 through 1936, the cumulative net loss was nearly $30,000,000. Additionally, arrears of more than $18,000,000 accumulated on the preferred stock.[8]

The company's future did not look any brighter under the presidency of Moses Pendelton, which lasted from 1936 until his death in 1950. During his first year in office, the firm lost $2,000,000. In 1937 the loss was $5,000,000. A casual observer could not help but wonder how much life there was behind the corporate facade of "the greatest name in woolens."

The next few years witnessed intermittent signs of life. As World War I had been a miracle for Wood, so too was World War II a windfall for Pendelton. Between 1939 and 1948, total profits were $88,000,000 "despite tax rates that would have made Billy Wood's hair curl."[9] Yet these relative successes could not alleviate the many problems besetting the textile corporation. Not even the Korean War years with their considerable profits from the sale of uniforms could save the aging hulk. In early 1955, amid bitter proxy fights, the once mighty American Woolen Company dramatically plunged beneath the waves as it merged with Textron, Incorporated of New York under the name of Textron American, Incorporated.[10]

In the years following Wood's death, while the ship he had launched was sinking, the American Woolen Company, the Old Colony Trust Company and Cornelius Ayer Wood, as executors and trustees of William M. Wood's estate, engaged in prolonged legal proceedings against one another. American Woolen charged William Wood with instances of breach of trust and fiduciary trust resulting in a loss to the firm of about $1,800,000. The trustees and executors filed counter-suits to recover some $2,000,000, which they had been obliged to pay as back income taxes on the salary of William Wood. In December 1931, after 106 days of actual trial, the cases were settled without the payment of money by any party except for $175,000 that Wood's widow paid to the American Woolen Company to help defray attorneys' fees.[11]

Although the Wood family emerged from this litigation relatively unscathed, they had not been so lucky two years earlier. In a far more costly trial, the United States Supreme Court, on June 3, 1929, decided the case of *Old Colony Trust et. al., Executors v. Commissioner of Internal Revenue.* The case revolved about the payment of Wood's income taxes by the American Woolen Company for the years 1919 and 1920. "The question in this case is, 'Did the payment by the employer constitute additional taxable income to such employee?' The answer must be 'Yes,'" wrote Chief Justice William Howard Taft in the majority opinion.[12] Wood's estate was ordered to pay the sum of $2,080,309 to the United States government for back taxes.

At the time of Wood's death, his surviving son, Cornelius, had "swapped considerable cash and most of his [William Madison Wood's] Shawsheen and West Andover real estate for the Park Square building in Boston."[13] Included

"Brick Shawsheen" today. Photograph of residential dwelling at 22 William Street, Shawsheen Village, Andover, Massachusetts. (Photograph by Annmarie Manzi)

in the sale to the Phillips Corporation of Maine (organized by J. Sumer Draper of Milton, Massachusetts) were the Post Office, the Spa, the Merchants' and Boys' Club buildings, Orlando Cottage, the Balmoral Playing Fields, the bowling green, and some 1500 acres in West Andover (Wood's extensive dairy farms). The purchase price of the Park Square structure, the largest office building in New England, was some $7,000,000.[14] With this single transaction, the Wood family gave up their considerable land holdings in Andover. Only the family estate Arden remained in their possession.

As for Shawsheen Village itself, the 231 residential units still owned by the American Woolen Company were sold in early July 1932 by the Textile Realty Company. The Andover-Shawsheen Realty Company, owned by F. M. and T. E. Andrew of Lawrence, Massachusetts, paid approximately $1,000,000 for the property.[15] On July 8, 1932, the new owners sent a letter to each of the tenants offering a non-transferable option to buy. Since 1932 was the worst year of the Great Depression, there were few takers. The Andrew letter promised:

> to maintain the same high standards that have kept Shawsheen Village so distinctive and choice a model community. . . . Future tenants will continue to be picked as before with a view to keeping this community on a high plane. Refinement has been the keynote since the beginning of the development and it will continue. For no reason will that air of distinction be allowed to disappear or even to diminish.[16]

"White Shawsheen" today. Photograph of residential dwelling at 8 Argyle Street, Shawsheen Village, Andover, Massachusetts. (Photograph by Annmarie Manzi)

William Wood surely would have approved of the elitist tone of this letter. Gradually, as the economy revived in the late 1930s, the residential properties passed to private owners, many of them former tenants.

The American Woolen Company, however, was still the reluctant possessor of the Executive Administration Building, the cafeteria, and the great Shawsheen Mill complex. Lionel Noah in 1935 dismissed Shawsheen Village by declaring, "[it's time] we got out of the real-estate business and back into manufacturing."[17] Wood's model corporate community—once the talk of the nation—had lasted a scant five years. Yet it was another quarter-century before American Woolen could bury this costly real estate venture in its company ledgers.

In 1945 a Roman Catholic teaching order, the Order of the Sacred Heart, purchased the office building for use as a boarding school. In 1956 the Raytheon Manufacturing Company purchased the abandoned Shawsheen Mill complex and cafeteria. Soon the mill buildings had a work force of 6,000 and a yearly payroll of $37,000,000. In the early 1970s, Raytheon built a much larger industrial park in West Andover and sold the Shawsheen property. Today, the sixty-year-old buildings house a score or more of diversified manufacturing concerns.

The Executive Administration Building has been converted to luxury apartments, but its exterior is unaltered. The Spa's outdoor dance pavilion has long since disappeared. Trains no longer stop at the Shawsheen Railroad

Depot. Acres of asphalt parking facilities surround the mill complex. Orlando Cottage is today the Lanam Club, an exclusive businessmen's dining club. Yet the sweeping Balmoral Playing Fields, now the property of the Town of Andover, still echo the shouts of soccer players and kite flyers. Algae has taken over Hussey's Pond, but the Shawsheen River still snakes its way through the village and canoeists and fishermen are again enjoying the stream.

The social structure of Shawsheen Village has continued to remain what it was from its inception—basically middle and upper middle class in composition. A casual perusal of recent Andover street listings reveals physicians, attorneys, professors, manufacturers, and corporate executives with Shawsheen Village addresses. There has always been a sprinkling of retired people in the community.

Of course, there have been changes in residential Shawsheen this past half-century. "White Shawsheen" is now multi-colored, but a surprisingly large number of home-owners continue the tradition of white houses with green shutters. One- and two-car garages have been built on most residential lots. Here and there, outdoor swimming pools and an occasional tennis court dot the landscape. The young saplings that were planted in the early 1920s are now full-grown oaks and maples lining the streets and forming an arbor effect in summer. A score or so of new residences have been constructed since 1924, most of them of Colonial Revival design, which blend harmoniously with Wood's original architectural theme.

On February 9, 1979, Shawsheen Village was designated an historic district and was accepted for inclusion in the National Register of Historic Places. William Madison Wood had built wisely and well. The far-sighted planning and execution that had gone into the creation of this corporate community were too valuable to remain in the dustbin of history.[18] Today, some sixty years after its inception, Shawsheen Village has gained the national attention it so well deserves.

APPENDIX A

List of American Woolen Company Mills, December 31, 1924

GROUPED BY STATES

Connecticut (3)

Elmville	Whitestone Mills
Moosup	Moosup (lower) Mills
	Glen Falls Mills

Kentucky (1)

Louisville	Bradford Mills

Maine (16)

Bridgton	Forest Mills
Dover	Brown Mills
Fairfield	Kennebec Mills
Foxcroft	Foxcroft Mills
Hartland	Hartland Mills
Madison	Indian Spring Mills
Newport	Newport Mills
North Vassalboro .	Vassalboro Mills
Oakland	Oakland Mills
Oldtown	Ounegan Mills
Pittsfield	Pioneer Mills
	Sebasticook Mills
	Sebasticook Mills Yarn Plant
	Waverly Mills
Skowhegan . . .	Arms Mills
	Anderson Mills

Massachusetts (22)

Andover	Shawsheen Mills
Blackstone . . .	Saranac Mills
Concord	Strathmore Worsted Mills
Dracut	Beaver Brook Mills
	Dracut Mills
Fitchburg	Arden Mills
	Beoli Mills
Franklin	Ray Mills
Lawrence	Ayer Mills
	Prospect Mills
	Washington Mills
	Wood Worsted Mills

Lowell	Bay State Mills
	Ram's Head Yarn Mills
Maynard	Assabet Mills
Medford	Riverina Mills
Plymouth	Puritan Mills
Rochdale	Rochdale Mills
South Royalston .	Royalston Mills
Uxbridge	Hecla Mills
Webster	Chase Mills
	Webster Mill

New Hampshire (5)

Dover	Sawyer Mills
Enfield	Baltic Mills
Lebanon	Lebanon Mills
	Mascoma Mills
Tilton	Tilton Mills

New York (2)

Fulton	Fulton Mills
Utica	Globe Mills

Rhode Island (8)

Harrisville	Anchor-Inman Mills
Pascoag	Anchor-Sheffield Mills
Manton	Manton Mills
Providence . . .	National and Providence Worsted Mills
	Valley Mills
	Weybosset Mills
Warren	Narragansett Worsted Mills

Vermont (3)

Ludlow	Black River Mills
Winooski	Burlington Mills
	Champlain Mills

60 Mills

133

APPENDIX B

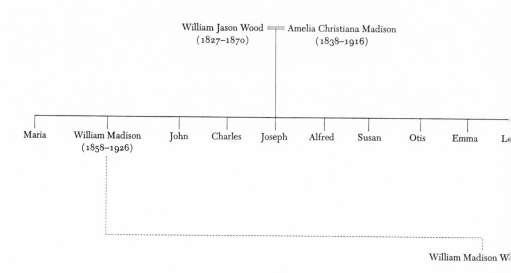

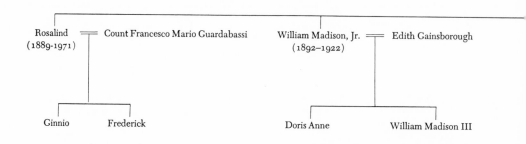

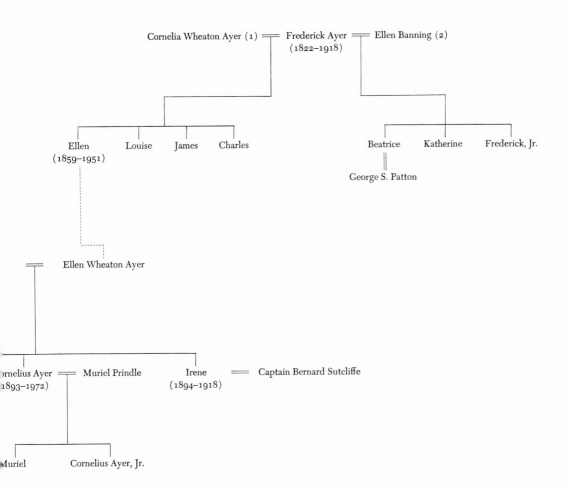

Cornelia Wheaton Ayer (1) ═══ Frederick Ayer ═══ Ellen Banning (2)
                                  (1822–1918)

Ellen   Louise   James   Charles   Beatrice   Katherine   Frederick, Jr.
(1859–1951)   ‖
                                                   George S. Patton

Ellen Wheaton Ayer

─rnelius Ayer ═══ Muriel Prindle   Irene   ═══ Captain Bernard Sutcliffe
─893–1972)   (1894–1918)

Muriel   Cornelius Ayer, Jr.

NOTES

CHAPTER I   Introduction *(pages 15–19)*

1 Richard Weiss, *The American Myth of Success* (New York: Basic Books, 1969), 3.
2 Allan Nevins, *Study in Power, John D. Rockefeller*, 2 vols. (New York: Charles Scribner's Sons, 1953), 1: 402; Weiss, 9.
3 Moses Rischin, ed., *The American Gospel of Success* (Chicago: Quadrangle Books, 1965), 9. See also William Miller, "American Historians and the Business Elite," *Journal of Economic History*, (Nov. 1949), 184–208. Miller's essay shows the role of historians in perpetuating the myth of rags to riches.
4 Rischin, 3.

CHAPTER II   Up the Ladder *(pages 21–43)*

1 *New Bedford Evening Standard*, February 3, 1926; *Boston Evening Transcript*, February 3, 1926.
2 Jason is probably the anglicized version of the name Jacinto. Madeira, which means "wood" in Portuguese, could also be the origin of the name Wood. This is admittedly a supposition, but a logical one according to Portuguese authorities. Author's conversation with Joseph A. Canha, official of the Portuguese Consulate, New Bedford, Massachusetts, July 1, 1981. Perhaps the young Portuguese immigrant took the name William Jason Wood in honor of an American benefactor. There were numerous Woods associated with the New Bedford whaling industry in the 1850s. If Wood shipped to America aboard a whaler, perhaps he took the name of a fellow crew member who had befriended him. A thorough search of official and unofficial records in Edgartown, Martha's Vineyard, Massachusetts where he spent his first five years in the United States, reveals not a single clue as to his Portuguese surname.
3 Certified copy of death certificate for Mrs. Amelia Christiana Wood, October 16, 1916, Woburn, Massachusetts. Her maiden name appears variously as Madison and Maderson in official records. To the assistant federal marshal who conducted the census of Edgartown, Martha's Vineyard, Massachusetts, on July 14, 1860, William Jason and Emma Wood (she used a variety of Christian names down through the years) dutifully reported their place of birth as Pico, the Azores.
4 A search of Records of Naturalization, Federal Records Center, Waltham, Massachusetts, for the 1860s reveals no such application for citizenship. A detailed examination of Massachusetts Superior Court records, Taunton Superior Court House, reveals no petition for naturalization.
5 Robin Bryans, *The Azores* (London: Faber & Faber, 1963), 146.
6 Pat Amaral, *They Ploughed the Seas* (St. Petersburg, Fla.: Valkyrie Press, Inc., 1978), xviii.
7 Alexander Starbuck, *History of the American Whale Fishery From Its Earliest Inception to the Year 1876*, 2 vols. (New York: Argosy, Antiquarian, Ltd., 1964), I: 506–07.
8 Letter from Richard C. Kugler, Director, Old Dartmouth Historical Society, Whaling Museum, New Bedford, to author, July 22, 1981.
9 Book 38, pages 99–101, Registrar of Deeds, Edgartown, Massachusetts. Courtesy Daniel F. Sullivan, Jr., July 10, 1981.
10 Starbuck, I: 506–07.
11 *New Bedford Evening Standard*, February 3, 1926.
12 Certified copies of baptismal records supplied author, courtesy of the Reverend Timothy Goldrick, St. Lawrence Rectory, New Bedford, Massachusetts, July 30, 1981.
13 Amaral, 160; *New Bedford Evening Standard*, February 3, 1926.
14 Keene Sumner, "A Business Genius Who Has Done What Others Said Was Impossible," *The American Magazine*, (June 1923), 203.

15 Amaral, 159.

16 Sumner, 203.

17 William Madison Wood interview, *New Bedford Evening Standard*, February 3, 1926.

18 Wood's school records and other documents provided the author through the courtesy of Paul Rodriguez, Superintendent of Schools, New Bedford, Massachusetts, July 24, 1981.

19 *New Bedford Evening Standard*, February 3, 1926.

20 *The NBIS* [New Bedford Institute for Savings] *Log*, January 1978, states that Wood purchased the building in 1918. He then conveyed the property to himself as trustee of the Arden Trust. "He planned to restore the building for use as a museum. His death prevented completion of the project. . . ."

21 Wood interview, *New Bedford Evening Standard*, February 3, 1926.

22 Sumner, 203.

23 Cornelius A. Wood (younger son of William Madison Wood), uncompleted and unpublished autobiography, Middlesex School, Concord, Massachusetts, 151. Hereafter referred to as CAW.

24 Sumner, 204.

25 John Bruce McPherson, "William Madison Wood: A Career of Romance and Achievement," *Bulletin*, National Association of Wool Manufacturers, (1926), 246–47. Hereafter referred to as *Bulletin*. *50th Annual Report of the American Woolen Company* (New York, 1948), 10. Latter report by courtesy of Granville K. Cutler, Andover, Massachusetts.

26 Wood interview, *New Bedford Evening Standard*, February 3, 1926.

27 Sumner, 204.

28 *50th Report*, 10.

29 Donald B. Cole, *Immigrant City: Lawrence, Massachusetts, 1845–1921* (Chapel Hill: University of North Carolina Press, 1963), Chp. II.

30 Maurice B. Dorgan, *History of Lawrence, Mass.* (published by the author, 1924), 44.

31 James H. Young, *The Toadstool Millionaires: A Social History of Patent Medicines in America before Federal Regulation* (Princeton University Press, 1961), 138–39, 140–41; James Cook Ayer entry, *American Biographical Dictionary* (New York: Charles Scribner's Sons, 1927), I: 450–51. There is a collection of Ayer's Almanacs at the University of Lowell, Lowell, Massachusetts.

32 Charles Cowley, *Reminiscences of James C. Ayer and the Town of Ayer* 3d ed. (Lowell, Mass., [1879]), 38. Cowley's exposure of the collapse of the Lawrence firm is based on confidential material supplied by James C. Ayer.

33 Frederick Ayer, *Reminiscences of Frederick Ayer* (Boston: privately printed, 1923; reprint ed., Redwood Press, 1971), Chp. 8.

34 Edward Mott Woolley, "Driving Forty Mills for $100,000 a Year," *McClure's* (August 1914), 126.

35 Ibid.

36 Ibid., 127.

37 F. Ayer, 72.

38 Ibid., 73.

39 CAW, 7–8.

40 Harold U. Faulkner, *Politics, Reform and Expansion; 1890–1900* (New York: Harper & Row, 1959), 145.

41 Ibid., xiii.

42 McPherson, "The American Woolen Company's Quarter-Century Record," *Bulletin* (October 1924), 473.

43 CAW, 4.

44 McPherson, "William Wood," *Bulletin* (1926), 248.

45 Woolley, 128.

46 Both woolen and worsted fabrics are made from the wool of the sheep. Woolens are made from the short fibers and are soft and rough-surfaced. Worsteds are made from the long fibers and are smooth and hard-surfaced. The reader's grandfather's overcoat was probably woolen, his suit probably worsted. So as not to confuse the reader, we refer to both woolens and worsteds as woolens. Also, all discussion of the woolen industry is based on woven and not on knitted woolen goods.

47 Faulkner, 75.

48 McPherson, "William Wood," *Bulletin* (1926), 249–50.

49 Woolley, 128.

50 Victor S. Clark, *History of Manufactures in the United States,* 3 vols. (1929; reprint ed., New York: Peter Smith, 1949), III: 205.

51 Ibid.; Arthur H. Cole, "A Neglected Chapter in the History of Combinations: The American Wool Manufacture," *Quarterly Journal of Economics* 37 (May 1923): 439.

52 Charles R. Flint entry, *Dictionary of American Biography,* 15 vols. (New York: Charles Scribner's Sons, 1964), XI: 305–06.

53 Orra L. Stone, *History of Massachusetts Industries: Their Inception, Growth and Success,* 2 vols. (Boston: The S. J. Clarke Publishing Co., 1930), II: 1510.; A. Cole, 440.

54 A. Cole, 441.

55 CAW writes: "Mr. Wood and Mr. Ayer together put through this plan and together owned all of the stock of the new company," 2.

56 F. Ayer, 75. Paul Cherington, *The Wool Industry, Commercial Problems of the American Woolen and Worsted Manufacture,* (Chicago: A. W. Shaw, 1916) is the best over-all treatment of the woolen textile industry in these years. Cherington, an Assistant Professor of Marketing, Graduate School of Business Administration, Harvard University, was an acknowledged authority in the field.

CHAPTER III   Paterfamilias *(pages 45–56)*

1 Bainbridge Bunting, *Houses of Boston's Back Bay* (Cambridge, Massachusetts: Harvard University Press, 1967), 217.

2 Ibid., 429.

3 "Arden." Andover Historical Society, "National Register Nomination" file.

4 Rosalind Wood later wrote an account of childhood life at Arden. This writer has drawn heavily upon it. It appears in CAW, 166–74.

5 CAW, 30.

6 CAW, 165, 167–68.

7 CAW, 83.

8 CAW, 80.

9 CAW, 108.

10 CAW, 332.

11 CAW, 162, 279. Cuttyhunk gossip has it that in 1904 when Wood first applied for membership in the exclusive Cuttyhunk Club, he was black-balled because he was Portuguese. By 1905 however, he was a member. He later bought the club and all its property for $100,000. "Dad's intention was to eventually own every house on the island. . . ." wrote CAW.

12 CAW, 155, 177.

13 CAW, 178.

14 CAW, 178.

15 CAW, 32.

16 CAW, 62.

17 CAW, 152.

18 Addison Mizner later described the incident to Henry Stephen Harvey, a young Palm Beach architect. Harvey, in turn, supplied the information to James R. Knott of West Palm Beach. The latter published the story "Right On Time," in the March–April 1980 issue of *Modern Living Magazine.* Mr. Knott supplied this writer with additional details in a letter dated August 21, 1980.

19 CAW, 80.

20 *Lowell Sun,* May 27, 1910.

21 CAW, 128.

22 CAW later wrote, "Dad offered it to me, but I really think he wanted Billy to have it," 180. At the time of the younger son's marriage, he was still an undergraduate at Harvard.

23 CAW, 180–81.

24 CAW, 170.

25 CAW, 110, 196, 272.
26 CAW, 150–51.
27 Ibid.
28 Andover Historical Society, *Newsletter* (Fall 1980), 3–4.
29 CAW, 177–78.
30 CAW, 163.
31 Claude M. Fuess, *Andover: Symbol of New England: The Evolution of a Town* (Andover, Mass.: The Andover Historical Society and The North Andover Historical Society, 1959), 391.
32 Thorstein Veblen, *The Theory of the Leisure Class* (New York: The New American Library, 1953), Chps. 3, 4, 5 passim.

CHAPTER IV   Empire Builder *(pages 57–81)*

1 *Fortune,* (April 1931), 71.
2 Stone, II: 1512–1515.
3 McPherson, "Quarter-Century Report," *Bulletin* (1924), 473–74; A. Cole, 442.
4 Woolley, 129.
5 Sumner, 208.
6 Sumner, 208.
7 Sumner, 208.
8 McPherson, "William Wood," *Bulletin* (1926), 256.
9 CAW, 154.
10 *Bulletin,* (1909), 523; CAW, 276.
11 *50th Annual Report,* American Woolen Company (New York, 1948), 12; A. Cole, 446.
12 McPherson, "Quarter-Century Report," *Bulletin* (1924), 484.
13 *50th Annual Report,* 13.
14 Dorgan, 53.
15 Woolley, 128.
16 McPherson, "Quarter-Century Report," *Bulletin* (1924), 477.
17 *Fortune,* (April 1931), 71; A. Cole, 441.
18 McPherson, "Quarter-Century Report," *Bulletin* (1924), 478.
19 The two best accounts of the Lawrence strike of 1912 are D. Cole, Chp. X and Henry F. Bedford, *Trouble Downtown: The Local Context of Twentieth-Century America* (New York: Harcourt Brace Jovanovich, 1978), Chp. I.
20 Sumner, 208.
21 Bedford, 15.
22 D. Cole, 6; Bedford, 18.
23 Melvyn Dubofsky, *We Shall Be All* (New York: Quadrangle, 1974), 235.
24 Robert E. Todd and Frank B. Sanborn, *The Report of the Lawrence Survey* (Lawrence, Mass., 1912), 258. This study, done in 1911, is commonly known as the White Report.
25 D. Cole, 72.
26 Todd and Sanborn, 37–38, 59–60, 87–89, 96, 105.
27 Bedford, 16.
28 D. Cole, 5.
29 Bedford, 17.
30 Bedford, 18.
31 Documentary Photo Aids, Phoenix, Arizona. Courtesy the Library of Congress.
32 D. Cole, 177.
33 *Complete History of Lawrence's Industrial Upheaval, 1912,* Collection of press clippings, Lawrence Public Library.
34 McPherson, "William Wood," *Bulletin* (1926), 251.
35 Bedford, 18.
36 Sumner, 208; *Bulletin,* (1919), 323–27. Frederick R. Edington was appointed the first head of the labor department. He was a close personal friend of William Jr.
37 *Bulletin,* (1919), 339–40; A. Cole, 452–53.
38 Woolley, 130; *American Wool and Cotton Reporter,* June 24, 1909, 873.
39 McPherson, "William Wood," *Bulletin* (1926), 253.

40 *50th Annual Report*, 15.

41 *Literary Digest*, "Woolen Industry to Hit H.C.L." [High Cost of Living], (January 3, 1920), 17.

42 McPherson, "Quarter-Century Report," *Bulletin* (1924), 479.

43 McPherson, "Quarter-Century Report," *Bulletin* (1924), 480.

44 Author's conversation with James Dalrymple, January 12, 1981. Dalrymple was Wood's personal bookkeeper and office manager from 1917 through 1924.

45 *50th Annual Report*, 14.

46 McPherson, "Quarter-Century Report," *Bulletin* (1924), 481.

47 *Bulletin*, (1916), 160–62; *Andover Townsman*, April 28, 1916.

48 *Lawrence Telegram*, February 5, 1926; CAW, 276. In 1909, Wood, in association with Joseph Koshland and Company, Boston wool merchants, built five ten-story warehouses on Sumner Street. See also, *Bulletin* (1909), 523.

49 McPherson, "Quarter-Century Report," *Bulletin* (1924), 481.

50 CAW, 289.

51 McPherson, "Quarter-Century Report," *Bulletin* (1924), 481; A. Cole, 451-52.

52 *Bulletin*, (1919), 124–25, 323–27; Sumner, 208. In connection with the group life insurance program, the underwriters, Traveler's Insurance Company, announced, "the policy is the largest group contract ever written, if not the largest insurance contract of of any kind," 125.

53 *Old Colony Trust Company, et al., Executors, v. Commissioner of Internal Revenue*, Supreme Court of the United States. October Term, 1928. Decided June 3, 1929. (279 U.S. 716, 49 S. Ct. 499); *Old Colony Trust Company and Cornelius Ayer Wood as Executors u/w of William M. Wood v. United States of America*, District Court of the United States, District of Massachusetts, Law No. 5958 June 16, 1936. (15 F. Supp. 417); *Fortune*, (April 1931), 72.

54 Clark, III: 343.

55 McPherson, "Quarter-Century Report," *Bulletin* (1924), 483.

CHAPTER V   Shawsheen Village: Dream Turned Reality *(pages 83–112)*

1 Frederic J. Osborn, *Green-Belt Cities* (New York: Schocken Books, 1969), 181. See also, William Ashworth, *The Genesis of Modern Town Planning* (London: Routledge and Kegan Paul Ltd., 1954), Chp. 8—"Approaches to Town Planning, 1909–1947"; and Roy Lubove, *The Urban Community: Housing and Planning in the Progressive Era* (Englewood Cliffs, N.J.: Prentice-Hall, 1967), 1–22.

2 A. W. [American Woolen] *Employee's Booster*, (September 1919); Cornelius A. Wood, "Your Home and You," (November 1922), 36–38. Lawrence Public Library. See also, Todd and Sanborn, 132–33, 135.

3 Clarence S. Stein, *Toward New Towns for America* (Cambridge, Mass.: M.I.T. Press, 1966), 12.

4 Stein, 16.

5 Fuess, 27.

6 John E. Pember, *Boston Sunday Herald*, December 12, 1920.

7 McPherson, "Shawsheen: Model Industrial Village," *Bulletin* (1924), 8.

8 McPherson, "Shawsheen," *Bulletin* (1924), 2.

9 *Shawsheen: The Model Community and the Home of the Offices and Staff of the American Woolen Co.* (Andover, Mass.: 1923). No pagination. Merrimack Valley Textile Museum.

10 Stone, *History*, II: 1517; Blueprint No. 1975–8, "Shawsheen Collection," Andover Historical Society.

11 In the single year of 1918 Wood purchased some 600 acres. McPherson, "Shawsheen," *Bulletin* (1924), 3. See also, CAW, 294.

12 It was in this region that Wood established American Woolen Company dairy farms on some 700 acres. Wood himself owned large tracts of land here, perhaps as much as 1500 acres.

13 *Andover Townsman*, October 3, 1919. The United States Post Office—Shawsheen Branch—officially opened for business on June 14, 1920.

14 Unnumbered blueprint (no date), "Shawsheen Collection," Andover Historical Society.

15 Author's conversation with the late Raymond "Dick" Hoyer, Andover, Mass., May 29, 1980. Mr. Hoyer was in charge of the maintenance of William Wood's personal limousines between 1920 and 1925. He was an employee of the Shawsheen garage in these years.

16 In smaller housing developments in Lowell, Lawrence, and Billerica, the Massachusetts Homestead Commission (created in 1911) patterned its design concepts on the English garden cities, e.g., Letchworth Avenue and Port Sunlight Road. Billerica's Burnham Road was named for the American city planner, Daniel H. Burnham, whose urban planning ideas were influential at the time. Shawsheen Village's Burnham Road was named for George L. Burnham, superintendent of the Almshouse. James Wallace, son of George M. Wallace, in a conversation with this writer, on July 28, 1981, confirmed his father's deep involvement in the building of Shawsheen Village. "As a youngster, I can recall Mr. Wood dropping by Aberfoyle [a large estate adjoining Arden, where the Wallace family lived] frequently, to have a cup of coffee and discuss building plans with my Dad." Joseph D. Knight, an executive of the American Woolen Company, also assisted Wood in constructing the model community. Author's interview with Mrs. Ernest Wilkinson, North Andover, Mass., August 18, 1981.

17 Hoyer interview, June 16, 1980.

18 *Andover Townsman*, November 16, 1923.

19 Stone, *History*, II: 1517.

20 *Architecture*, (March 15, 1912), 33, observed that Colonial Revival "should be the accepted type of design for public or semi-public buildings in our own small American towns, especially in the East, where colonial traditions still survive with some strength."

21 Garage attendants delivered the cars to the owners' homes in the morning and picked them up in the evening. Only the residents of "Brick Shawsheen" were offered this service, for which there was a monthly charge.

22 The fifty-cent charge in each monthly rental was to cover the cost of the sunken metal garbage containers at the rear of each of the houses. Once the container was paid for, the fifty-cent charge was eliminated. Dalrymple interview, July 17, 1975. Mr. and Mrs. Dalrymple lived in "White Shawsheen" in these early years.

23 The general grocery store was operated by the Shawsheen Market, Inc., a subsidiary of the American Woolen Company. McPherson, "Shawsheen," *Bulletin* (1924), 5.

24 Fuess, 390.

25 *Andover Townsman*, July 29, 1921.

26 The creamery received its dairy products from the large dairy farms of the American Woolen Company in West Parish, Andover. Dairy products were also supplied to the firm's restaurants in Lawrence.

27 Hoyer interview, June 16, 1980.

28 Wood's 1923 promotional brochure (cited in note 9 above) carried a photograph of the Boy's Club with the caption "An Exact Replica of Washington's Valley Forge Headquarters." Perhaps this was the origin of the local legend.

29 *Andover Townsman*, June 1, 1923.

30 Village children above the sixth grade were obliged to attend the Stowe School in Andover.

31 *Andover Townsman*, February 9, 1923.

32 *Andover Townsman*, September 1, 9, November 17, 1922. See also notes of the Andover School Committee, dated February 6, 1923, and March 2, 1923, office of the Superintendent of Schools, Andover. These notes contain Wood's letter offering a five-acre site for the school.

33 Fuess, 421–22.

34 *Fortune*, (June 1935), 68.

35 Building costs in the United States had almost doubled between 1914 and 1924. Stein, 21.

36 *Andover Townsman*, June 19, 1925.

37 *Andover Townsman*, February 11, 1921.

38 Andover Historical Society, "Shawsheen Collection." The 1924 edition of the directory may have been the only one published, since no others have been found.

39 *Andover Townsman,* October 24, 1924.
40 *Andover Townsman,* February 18, 1921.
41 *Andover Townsman,* March 14, 1924.
42 Fuess, 426. Fuess also stated that Cochran and Wood were both "impulsive, impatient, imaginative, irritated by opposition, and stubbornly persistent . . . autocratic. . . . Each in some moods seemed mad, but it was the madness of genius," 424.

CHAPTER VI   Wood's Final Years: Triumphs Beget Tragedies *(pages 113–125)*

1 *Fortune,* (June 1935), 67.
2 *Fortune,* (June 1935), 67.
3 *Fortune,* (June 1935), 68–70.
4 Samuel L. Powers, *Portraits of a Half Century* (Boston: Little Brown, 1925), 206–11. Powers' statistics appear, not in his study of Wood, but in the *Lawrence Sunday News,* February 7, 1926.
5 *Fortune,* (June 1935), 132.
6 *Fortune,* (April 1931), 110.
7 *Fortune,* (April 1931), 110.
8 *Fortune,* (March 1954), 72.
9 *Fortune,* (April 1931), 94; A. Cole, 452.
10 *Fortune,* (June 1935), 67.
11 A. Cole, 467.
12 *Fortune,* (April 1931), 94.
13 CAW, 274.
14 *New York Journal of Commerce and Commercial Bulletin,* June 14, 1920; *New York Times,* February 3, 1926.
15 *Andover Townsman,* June 18, 1920.
16 *Old Colony Trust Company and Cornelius Ayer Wood . . . v. United States of America,* June 16, 1936, 821.
17 *Old Colony . . . v. Commissioner of Internal Revenue,* June 3, 1929, 408.
18 *Old Colony . . . v. United States of America,* June 16, 1936, 818.
19 *Andover Townsman,* August 18, 1922; *New York Times,* October 11, 1922. Massachusetts Register of Motor Vehicles blamed A. H. Earle, driver of the car William Jr. swerved to avoid, for the latter's death.
20 CAW, 282.
21 CAW, 282.
22 *New York Times,* November 28, 1922.
23 CAW, 290.
24 CAW, 291.
25 CAW, 287, 288, 289.
26 CAW, 289.
27 *Lawrence Tribune,* February 3, 1926.
28 *New York Times,* April 25, 1924.
29 *Andover Townsman,* August 15, 1924.
30 CAW, 291.
31 *Andover Townsman,* January 1, 1925.
32 *Boston Post,* February 3, 1926.
33 *Boston Post,* February 3, 1926.
34 *Boston Post,* February 3, 1926; author's interviews with Mrs. Ernest Wilkinson, August 18, 1981 and James Dalrymple, January 12, 1981; *Fortune,* (June 1935), 68.
35 CAW, 294. A Lawrence workers' magazine, *Lawrence Labor,* in its July 27, 1923 issue described Shawsheen Village as "Suckersville." *Lawrence Labor* collection, State Historical Society of Wisconsin, Madison, Wisconsin.
36 *Boston Post,* February 3, 1926.
37 CAW, 287, 288, 289.
38 CAW, 291.
39 *Boston Post,* February 3, 1926.
40 *Boston Globe,* February 3, 1926.

41 CAW, 293.

42 CAW, 288.

43 *New York Times*, February 3, 1926.

44 Of the dozens of obituaries that have been examined by the author, those which appeared in *New Bedford Evening Standard, Boston Post* and *New York Times*, February 3, 1926, were the most informative and historically accurate.

45 *New Bedford Evening Standard*, February 3, 1926.

46 Marcus L. Hansen, *The Problem of the Third Generation Immigrant* (Rock Island, Ill.: Augustana Historical Society, 1938), 8.

47 D. Cole, 195–96; *Lawrence Evening Tribune*, May 9, 1924.

48 *New York Times*, May 1, 1919.

49 *New Bedford Evening Standard*, February 3, 1926.

50 Joseph Frazier Wall, *Andrew Carnegie* (New York: Oxford University Press, 1970), 806–07.

51 *Old Colony Trust Company and Cornelius Ayer Wood . . . v. United States of America*, June, 16, 1936, 823.

CHAPTER VII   Afterward *(127–132)*

1 *50th Annual Report*, 13.

2 *Fortune*, (June 1935), 125.

3 *Fortune*, (March 1954), 94.

4 *Fortune*, (June 1935), 125; *Moody's Analysis of Investments and Security Rating Books: Industrial Investments* (New York: Moody's Investor's Service, 1922), CLXXV; *Moody's Manual of Investments: Industrial Securities* (New York: Moody's Investor's Service, 1933), A4, 114–15.

5 *Fortune*, (April 1931), 96; *Fortune*, (June 1935), 126; *Bulletin*, (1931), 34–35.

6 *Fortune*, (June 1935), 128.

7 *Fortune*, (March 1954), 94.

8 *Fortune*, (June 1935), 126.

9 *Fortune*, (March 1954), 94.

10 *Bulletin*, (1954), 1–59, 1–63; the *New York Times Index* (1954) devotes four-and-one-half columns (55–56) to references to the bitterness of the struggle.

11 *Old Colony Trust . . . v. United States of America*, June 16, 1936, 819. See also, *Fortune*, (April 1931), 72.

12 *Old Colony Trust . . . v. Commissioner Internal Revenue*, June 3, 1929, 408. Apparently the statute of limitations had prevented the I.R.S. from including Wood's 1918 salary in the suit.

13 CAW, 277; *Andover Townsman*, April 2, 1926.

14 *Andover Townsman*, April 2, 1926.

15 *Andover Townsman*, July 8, 1932.

16 *Andover Townsman*, July 8, 1932.

17 *Fortune*, (June 1935), 131.

18 The following excerpt is from a letter written by Larry Richards, member of the architectural faculty, University of Toronto, Canada, to Vincent Scully, professor of art history, Yale University, September 17, 1975. Copy of the letter was supplied to the author by Professor Richards. ". . . Recently, I was exposed to an interesting research project being coordinated by a friend . . . He is documenting and evaluating Shawsheen Village, a planned woolen mill community built in the early 1920's. . . . Surprisingly, no thorough books or dissertations have been done on Shawsheen Village, and [Ed's] project may help to save it from unimaginative developer plans. I'm telling you all of this because I hope that you or one of your students might be interested in learning more about . . . Roddy's work. Shawsheen should, I feel, be protected and rejuvenated. It offers a superb framework for what one hopes would be some kind of sensitive growth. . . . That the nation's architectural and urban planning journals, have, over the past sixty years, failed to examine the origins of Shawsheen Village, is, to say the least, surprising."

INDEX